care 360°

A HANDBOOK FOR CAREGIVING TO YOUR PARENT

DEBRA LaCoppola

Copyright © 2022 by Debra LaCoppola

No part of this publication may be reproduced, stored in a retrieval system or transmitted in any form or by any means, electronic, mechanical, photocopying, recording, scanning or otherwise, except as permitted under Sections 107 or 108 of the 1976 United States Copyright Act, without the prior written permission of the Publisher. Requests to the publisher for permission should be addressed to **360parentcare.com**

Limit of Liability/Disclaimer of Warranty: The Publisher and The Author make no representations or warranties with respect to the accuracy or completeness of the content of the work and specifically disclaim all warranties, including without limitations warranties of fitness for a particular purpose. No warranty may be created or extended by sales or promotional materials.

The advice and strategies contained herein may not be suitable for every situation. This work is sold with the understanding that the publisher is not engaged in rendering medical, legal or other professional advice or services. If professional assistance is required, the services of a competent professional person should be sought. Neither the publisher or the author shall be liable for damages arising herefrom. The fact that an individual organization or website is referred to in this work as a citation and/or potential source of further information does not mean that the author or the Publisher endorses the information the individual, organization or website may provide or recommendations they/it may make. Further, readers should be aware that Internet websites listed in this work may have changed or disappeared between when this work was written and when it is read.

For general information please refer to **360parentcare.com**
Cover Design by **Gloria Nadelcu**
Doodle Illustrations by **Kyle Tezak**
Icons - **TheNounProject.com**
Formatting by **Charles Meier**

ISBN 979-8-218-07266-7
Printed in the United States of America

Contents

INTRODUCTION 01

MEET THE CAREGIVERS 08

PART ONE

FILLING THE WELL: SELF CARE FIRST 30

CALM 38
Presence 39
Mantra 40
Meditation 43
Journaling 46
Trust Yourself 48

NOURISH 54
Nutrition 56
Green Juice 57
Hydrate 60

CONNECT 64
Nature Heals 65
Movement Heals 67
Yoga 71
Reading 75
Friends 77
Gratitude + Perspective 79

SOUND REST 82
Sleep 83
Bedroom Sanctuary 85
Napping 91

Part Two

Fueled & Ready: Connected Caregiving 96

It Happens In Stages 97

Is My Home Ready? 102
Driving 104
Mobility. 107
Bathroom. 111
Daily Routines 118

The Support Squad 128
Building Your Team 129
Budget 132
Form The Team 133
Boundaries. 142

Budget & Finances 152

Advocacy 162
Medications 164
Dignity + Deep Listening 167

Nursing Homes & Care Facilities 174
The Staff 177
Facility Evaluation Criteria 178
Food 179
Intuition & Gut Feelings 181

The Hospital 184
Nurse Relations 185
HR & Finance Departments 188
Directives + Living will 191
Hospital Food 194
Visit, Visit, Visit 196

From The Heart 198
Enrichment 203
Resentment, Joy & Forgiveness 208
Saying Goodbye 215

ACKNOWLEDGMENTS
AND
IMMENSE GRATITUDE TO...

- ✦ Charles Meier, my husband, for being the rock that my father, Lenny, and I each needed in more ways than we can count.
- ✦ My brother, Angelo, for being Dad's favorite. Your relationship was inspiring.
- ✦ Elia, for your guidance and friendship.
- ✦ Laurie, for countless hours of yoga classes.
- ✦ Rachel, for selflessly cleaning and shopping while getting your real estate license.
- ✦ Dad's friend, Michael, whom he met at church and adopted as a surrogate son.
- ✦ Cindy, Jimmy, and Sinead—for being there till the end. I am forever grateful.
- ✦ All the amazing friends and family that provided bits of wisdom when I needed it.
- ✦ My lovely mother-in-law, Faith, for your love *of* and care *for* Lenny.
- ✦ My father-in-law, Charles, who made Dad feel so loved and welcome.
- ✦ Everyone that took care of Lenny at the nursing home and beyond: his nurses and aides, Miss Shutes, Mr. Paul, and Nurse Roseanne - Thank you, he loved you all.
- ✦ The Incredible contributors who allowed me to interview you for this book. I know how painful it was to recount and re-live some portions, so, *thank you* from the bottom of my heart: Susan, Lexie, Amber, Penelope, Tyler, Erin and Valerie.
- ✦ My amazing editor, Lori Stevens, who made this book sing! I'm so glad I manifested you.

And finally, thank you, Lenny and Barbara, for bringing me into the world with all your love. You are in my heart every waking day. I love you both so deeply.

Foreward

Care 360° is a powerful and transformational guidebook to living life as your best expression. Debra brilliantly teaches us first how to fill our own self-care well, so we are brimming with the nourishment needed for us to show up and do our best work. And once we have that strong foundation, she guides us into being the most effective, compassionate, and dedicated caregiver we can be. As a caregiver myself, I know first-hand that it's easy to run out of fuel & patience as each day unfolds. But, this magnificent treasure trove of deep insights and real-world guidance provides the perfect blueprint to helping, serving & taking care of others, as you help and heal yourself.

-davidji, author of Sacred Powers

Introduction

WELCOME. You are here because you're caring for your mom or dad who can't do everything they used to do. Maybe you've noticed changes in their cognitive behavior? Or perhaps one of these reflects your parent's current circumstances:

- ✦ They got sick and you're helping them get back on their feet.
- ✦ They can still get around, but their health is declining.
- ✦ They are very ill, bed-bound, or in-and-out of the hospital.
- ✦ They reside in a nursing home or 24-hour care facility.
- ✦ Or, they may already be in hospice care, very close to the end of their lives.

Whatever your situation, I understand how hard it is. I went through all these steps and stages with my own parents. Each stage felt different than the one before it. Each was just as confusing, painful, and difficult, some even lonely. Whatever the stage, we all have a unique journey. This is an ever-changing time so be prepared for change to come often—sometimes daily.

My goal in creating this guide is to help you maintain balance while navigating the responsibilities of caregiving for a parent, so you are also cared for in the process.

Despite the many difficulties, there is also a sweetness in caregiving for a parent: you love them so much yet this will likely be the last time you get to spend with them, your final memories.

Self-care while caregiving is a subject people don't talk about-much— (not surprising, considering the state of the healthcare industry.) Most individuals tend to the demands of caregiving at the expense of every other life alarm. Personal problems are pushed under the rug until the caregiver becomes broken themselves. Only then does attention switch over to try to fix the personal issues, often too late. Society offers no real prevention assistance, either. As a result, caregivers have nothing in place to support us before our own 'breaking' happens.

This is the core tenet of the first 180° of Care: Self-care is not selfish.

I repeat, **self-care is not selfish**. It is quite the opposite. We give better care when we attend to our own needs, first. I said that and I mean it.

Early in the book, a concept of "filling the well" is introduced, meaning, preparing yourself not to become sick or depleted while giving your all caring for your parent. We can't give when our tanks are empty. Repeat this often and remind yourself daily: you *must* nourish and fill your personal well with love, care, nutritional meals, and proper rest, all while reducing your stress levels. You may be the best caregiver in the world, but if you don't give that same attention and care to yourself, your *consistent best* is impossible. Think *mind, body, and spirit.*

I am here to guide you how to put things in place to not run on empty, so the first thing I will emphasize is: It's not easy. Every day is not a walk in the park. But if you put a few good practices in place, this journey will have some rewarding moments. Your caregiving will feel as though it is an act of love, not survival.

Know that you will look back on this time for many years to come—probably the rest of your life. Once I began to think of caregiving as my 'service work,' I understood my role in a much more proactive way. You're in the middle of caregiving right now, and when you're in it, you probably don't see it this way. Those mixed feelings and sadness after your parent passes will be overtaken by the pride you'll hold deep within. Pride in having stood up and taken charge: You gave of yourself while giving care to someone you love.

Hang on. Don't give up.

I still experience daily gratitude for being able to provide my dad, Lenny, the level of care I did. Yet occasionally, instead of thinking: *I can't believe I pulled off all those years balancing a photography career, my home and marriage, PLUS caregiving at the highest possible level to Dad;* I find my mind hijacked by darker thoughts such as, *I could have done this better… or that differently…* Or the worst: *Did I do enough?*

Then I stop myself.

I remind myself of all those times I talked myself off the ledge: *"You are only human, Debra—not a saint, not a machine—you are only human and you, my dear, are doing the BEST job you can. So why aren't I thanking myself instead? OK, yes, this is difficult. Yes, caregiving is hard work. Just remember, anything that requires giving so much time and attention alongside love IS hard, yet here I am, doing it!"*

So, then I'd pat myself on the back, look in the mirror and say out loud, *"I am Strong! I am BRAVE! I've GOT THIS! Now let's go!"*

Uncertainty about how long your caregiving role will last is another hurdle. What lasts months for some might end up ten years' commitment (or more) for others. My advice? G-o. S-l-o-w-l-y. This book helps you learn to rest properly, eat nutritiously, stay hydrated, breathe, move, meditate, form a support team, and take pauses to appreciate yourself knowing you're the best caregiver you may be. No matter what you think, you're doing it right. Put just a few of these tips into practice and you will see long into the future how giving *to* yourself while giving *of* yourself helped lighten the burden.

As a professional photographer for over 25 years, it took over a decade before I recognized my own experience combining self-care with caregiving that I carried into every shoot. I was intuitively doing that until a cathartic exchange occurred while I was staying at the Kripalu Center for Yoga in Massachusetts on an extended assignment shooting senior yogis, healers and meditation leaders at the institute. It was a beautiful senior yogi's turn to step in front of my camera for her portrait series. Just as we started, tears began streaming down both of our faces at the same moment, so I stopped shooting.

"Wow," I said, taken back.

"Wow," she mirrored.

We embraced in a big, tight hug before she looked me in the eye and said, "Do you know that you channel the individuals you are photographing"?

"No," I said. "I don't even know what that means."

To this day I recall her explanation: "You connect to each person at their level, giving of yourself and holding your space totally open for your subjects to be themselves. You fully honor *our* whole experience instead of forcing us to follow your plan. What a gift."

My oh my, I had no idea! I *did* know that whoever is in front of my camera gets my love and undivided attention, but to learn that my shooting style had such an impact? I mean, let's face it, some dread having their picture taken, but to hear my approach comes across as nurturing others' self-expression... Well, that exchange made me realize I needed to make my balancing act *intentional*. Balancing self-care with acts of service was serious; it is my career!

As of that moment, I *knew* I was truly lucky. Photography wasn't only a talent I've *loved, loved, loved* since age 7, it is also *supposed to be* my life's work—what I am truly meant to do! My destiny... my *dharma*. "Holding space" for people so they may feel empowered to openly express themselves requires surrendering my ego and agenda. This can only happen because I honor myself through my preparation rituals a few days before each shoot. That resulting energy reserve enables me to fully serve them during our sessions. It's the same as caregiving.

Her comment helped me create a more conscious ritual before every photo shoot. Now in the few days leading up, I intentionally rest up, eat well, meditate, and do yoga. On the day of the shoot, I remind myself: *This opportunity isn't about me. It's about them, now. I am only here for (them.)*

It may sound woo-woo, but part of why I love life so much is rooted in my belief there is something we are each here to do. Once I re-classified my professional talents as 'service work,' I saw how giving *to* myself meant receiving tenfold payback. Now, I'm best able to serve when I honor my own needs first whether career, family, or friends. Call it 'filling the well' so to speak.

I use the same method and mantras to keep me present in each moment while in service. The practice readies me for any magic about to happen. "Magic?" you ask. Yes. You will find caregiving has magical moments as well. There are no good days without challenging days; but throughout that pain and sadness comes moments of immense joy. My only hope for writing this handbook is that others find that same peace I found while caregiving—the profound transformation that my dad and I went through as life unfolded for us together.

Strive for **Balance**: the key to successful self-care while caregiving. That's why this handbook is arranged to easily flip between the guidance and tips in the **front half** for **self-care** and the **back half** for **caregiving**. Skip around the sections to find the topics most relevant for your needs in each moment. Not all the content may apply to everything you experience, or in the order presented, so you must learn to trust and love yourself and follow your intuition. It's all in here – well, most anyway.

I'm so honored that you're here—that you found this handbook. I really hope it helps people in ways I am unaware of. I wish it had existed for me.

Sending you lots of love on your journey. *-DLC*

Meet The Caregivers

Throughout this book you will find portions of interviews with seven very different women that were (or still are) the caregiver for a parent. Each is extraordinary in how they manage(d) their caregiving role in whatever unique way each circumstance created. A common thread shared throughout is **compassion**: for their parents and for themselves.

**Dr. Penelope Potter
on her own Journey as well as
being caregiver to mom, Josephine**

One look at my 'work-clothes' through the years sums up my preparation for the role of caregiver: pink-and-white-striped apron in the 50's. Blue-and-white skirt with a pinafore and white cap around the back of the head in the 60's. Switch to navy culottes with white blouse and exercise mat for the 70's. Then, a white jacket with a stethoscope around my neck into the 80's. Eventually came an opportunity to 'change my clothes'—those doctor clothes I'd worn so long.

Out of exhaustion and depression, I took a 'Leave-of-Absence', (a misnomer of a phrase. 'Leave-for-Presence' better describes that three-month yoga retreat in the mountains of British Columbia.)

There I was, that twelve-week heart-rest, a true Sabbatical: Absent to the world: Present to my heart. During one workshop on *the purpose of life*, each attendee was asked to describe a 'typical day' in their lives. The audience listened quietly while I rambled through my day job, finishing that I always conclude late in the evening reading the heart EKGs of patients. The room was silent until the director gently asked, "And what does YOUR heart's EKG say, Penelope?"

I was speechless.

The rest is history, so to speak. Many changes followed but from 1983 to this beautiful, present moment, I have never ceased the inward journey that infuses my 'outward' journey with purpose, patience, and peace. I re-focused my work on slow and quiet patients: the aging and dying who seemed more comforted by my slow and quiet care. That same slow and quiet care eventually came to include my dear mother.

It really was such a blessing for all of us that we were able to be with my mother and she could remain in her home. At the start, my husband Tom was a doctor facing a new, difficult commute from my mother's house. Meanwhile, I was home-schooling my daughter, Suji, while looking after my mom during the day and managing her pain at night. It became almost impossible for Tom to continue the new routine, so we switched it up for him to come to my mother's house every night after work for dinner to eat as a family. Afterwards, he went back to our own home while my daughter and I stayed with Mom. That went on about five months until she passed.

Perhaps the secret/not-so-secret to my peace and happiness today is my daughter, now a nurse at the University Hospital near me. I also enjoy my small garden with a strawberry patch, and one-eyed cat named Lilly-Bee who sits on me for five minutes before it's time to get up for meditation. (On some days I even thank her.) Lest we forget the hundreds of trees planted, hundreds of miles hiked, and thousands of hugs and Thank You's I always offer to my beloved Mother Earth and all Her darling children...

I pray for the well-being of all the world. **Om Lokah Samastah Sukhino Bhavantu.**

**Susan Wilber,
caregiver to mom, Clarice**

As President of her own company with more than thirty years in the wine, restaurant & culinary industry, Susan Wilber has been featured in *The New York Times, Wine & Spirits, Wine Enthusiast, New York Magazine, The New York Post* and *BizBash*. Her resume roles include Sommelier and General Manager of the world-famous restaurant, Lutèce; Culinary Producer for the James Beard Foundation Awards; and quite a few more eyebrow-raising achievements under her professional belt.

But that rich and accomplished career trajectory did little to prepare her for the unfamiliar terroir of caregiver. Susan graciously shares morsels of her caregiving story arc with us throughout CALM, NOURISH, and BUILDING SUPPORT sections.

Her take:
I had a suspicion that something had been changing with my mom before any medical confirmation. During my weekly phone calls from New York, I noticed our conversations were becoming the same. We talked about the weather, then I would ask all the questions. She'd respond but didn't really instigate dialogue. There were a few minor hints in her behaviors, but we never really discussed any changes in her mental state.

Then my mom fell down a flight of stairs and broke her hip. In the hospital, my brother mentioned she had been drinking a lot, so we let the anesthesiologist know (in case there was a risk of high alcohol content in her blood.) We also questioned changes in her cognitive abilities and requested a mini-mental exam. Sure enough, the diagnosis was early dementia. Her fall brought everything into focus for the next ten years.

Caregiving to Mom was very different at the start than how it progressed. Early on she lived with my brother because flying back and forth from NY to Atlanta was difficult for me. Eventually, my brother and I wanted something different: him, to keep our mother in her home, but I knew this wasn't the right choice. That tension lasted for 5 years. In the end, he was run down, fed up, and had gone thru all his resources—then promptly dumped the matter into my lap. That's when I became the main caregiver from afar in NY (another mess, financially and emotionally, since I was the one left negotiating my mother out of her own house and into assisted living.)

It was a journey involving many different levels of caregiving. To suddenly be responsible for my parent was complicated—a real adjustment. Having been single and caring for only myself up to that point was a weird role-reversal that messed with my psyche. And losing your parent, there's an incredible amount of grief to process too.

**Amber Henderson,
caregiver to mom, Lorraine**

Amber was living in New York City working as an esthetician and make-up artist when COVID hit. At the time, she figured a temporary move back to where she grew up in New Orleans might be beneficial for both her mother and herself. At the time of this writing, she remains her mom's caregiver in NOLA.

Amber emphasizes keeping things light to help maintain sanity and composure. Her sage advice pops up in **Self-Care's** CALM chapter and throughout the **Caregiving** chapters. How she ended up a caregiver, in her words:

As an only child, I was the sole person checking in on my mom in New Orleans during COVID while living in New York. At the time, she was still a housekeeper–even at 78 years old. (She had been housekeeping and taking care of children and families since she was 18.)

While technically retired by 65, Mom needed extra money for living expenses as being employed as a domestic all her life meant her social security only covered her rent. Besides, she adored her work, having remained with the same families for many years.

Once I got back home, I realized my mom didn't understand what was going on with COVID. She wasn't even sure why I was home. As it happened, I started reaching out to her primary care doctors and that's when I found out she had been missing appointments. Once I finally took her to the doctor to get checked and back on track, I was told she had dementia.

Unfortunately, after Hurricane Katrina my mom's brother and sister moved farther out, about two hours away. And they have their own health issues, which means we don't have the support of anyone else close by.

**Lexie Hallahan,
caregiver to parents, Doris & George**

A registered dietician & dedicated athlete, Lexie was living in Hawaii when she simultaneously fell in love with surfing and her husband, Tom. Both serious surfers, Lexie and Tom then decided to move back to her home state of Oregon and landed on the coast near the best surfing spot where they became immersed in a whole surfing-centric community. In the spring of 2005, Lexie and an inspired and talented team of surf instructors launched **NW Women's Surf Camps,** which create surfing opportunities for individuals in the Northwest to broaden their horizons, expand their lives, and deepen their connection with the ocean via the transformations that only surfing offers. Their surfing camps host mindfulness lessons, yoga clinics and provide yummy and nutritious meals, (the best tuna curry sandwiches you'll ever eat.) Events are anchored to a vision of an inclusive world that is non-judgmental, understanding and respectful. She and her thriving Pacific Northwestern women's surfing community are even creating surf sister-ships that cross borders which they hope to expand for decades to come. **nwwomenssurfcamps.com**

Lexie's inspirational contributions are strong examples of how caring for oneself needs to be Priority One. She credits being an avid surfer and her love of natural settings as providing the necessary support for coping skills to get her through her difficult journey. Her self-care advice is woven throughout the handbook.

My mother had a nervous breakdown when I was seven years old. We somehow managed, but then Dad took on a big new management job, I just remember my mother was mentally ill the first few years Dad was on this new job. In the late 80's, a new breakthrough drug came up that dramatically helped my mother re-engage and the two of them could go out to dinner and meet up with friends again. They started having more of a normal life until out of the blue, Dad got sick with a rare blood disease and was diagnosed with only a year to live. I immediately became Dad's caregiver and took him to every doctor's appointment, helping Mom as best I could.

Dad refused to go through the rigorous treatments required of his condition or "die that way," (his words,) so as predicted, he lived only that one final year.

A decade or so passed, but once I turned 39, I started caring for Mom for what was to become a total of fourteen years. The hardest part was that she just kept mentally deteriorating. My biggest caregiving lesson was about my own self-care: when my well isn't full—meaning I'm not getting the best nutrition, rest, doing my yoga, being out in natural settings—if I skipped all those things, I could not be present when visiting Mom.

When operating on "autopilot," I got frustrated—couldn't even function properly. But with a 'full well' (rested, nourished, and personal time doing activities that I enjoy), I was able to be there with a much more positive mindset. I learned firsthand that Presence makes life a more tolerable, richer experience. In the end, my self-care allowed my mother to feel the most cared for.

**Erin Hyland,
caregiver to dad, Dennis**

Born and raised in the beautiful Coachella Valley, Erin is a true desert local. Her passion for volunteering has served many boards of directors and desert causes: *the Junior League, Desert Advertising Federation, Cathedral City PACE (Parks & Community Events Commission,) Joyfully Grieving,* as well as Coachella Valley orgs *'Collaborative', 'Leadership', & 'Women Leaders Forum.'* Besides those, one might also try the *Humane Society of the Desert's Orphan Pet Oasis* where she regularly volunteers. She lives in Cathedral City with her rescues: pup, Tessa, and CeCe the calico cat.

Erin's words of encouragement are especially peppered throughout **Self-Care** to inspire all caregivers with her positive mental attitude and pure love for her parents. Her bittersweet experiences in her words:

Once I graduated college, I built an enjoyable life for myself in San Diego and wanted to stay. Then my dad—only 47 years old—got sick. He started having fainting spells, which was pretty odd because he was super active in sports, did physical labor for a living, and was in general good health. But now, he would just suddenly faint in the middle of his kitchen. Once, he hit his head so hard, he went to the hospital. The medical staff couldn't figure out what was wrong until some unusual tests discovered a rare cancer in his bile duct (cholangional carcinoma) which required surgery and chemo to shrink the tumor.

Fast-forward nine or so years, Dad was still alive and under the care of both my mom and me. Then I suffered a major car accident and Mom became our dual-caregiver for six months.

Erin's story continues later in Handbook...

**Val Griffin,
caregiver to mom, Helen**

A passionate force for life, Val has no shortage of roles: entrepreneur, radio personality, baker, author, Word of God teacher, SoCal realtor, and mom to Chanel. She and her daughter are animal lovers who own and ride horses. Val shares wonderful advice in both the **Self-Care** and **Caregiving** sections of the book. A synopsis of her story in her own words:

My parents had been married for almost 60 years when my father passed of cancer. He was the love of my mother's life. Around 90 years old, mom was still living alone, so I started to cook all her meals. I would make a whole week's worth of food to bring over.

Suddenly, without telling me, she began to think there was too much salt in the food... then too much fat... then she began to throw out all the uneaten food— which meant my mom wasn't eating.

That was about the time I saw some changes in her thinking and knew something wasn't right. As a result, I left my own home to move into the big house with Mom—the house I hadn't lived in since I was a teenager. Once I was living with her, I noticed her frailty and confirmed that her eating patterns were off.

I started taking her to doctor appointments for blood pressure issues which devolved into decreasing kidney functions, but because most conditions were related to her diet, we were able to turn things around. We weren't dealing with illness other than hypertension, which we controlled with diet and medication once I lived with her.

My Mom lived as long as she wanted. She was 95 when she passed. We wanted her to live longer but she told us she "loved us but was old and tired, and needed us to understand that." I'm glad that she had that victory.

My mother was always thanking me—not everyone receives that, but you, yourself, have to believe that you did the best job you could do. *You* know.

My sister was also appreciative. She told me "You were the one chosen for this, Valerie." And she was right. I'm glad I was the one because it leaves an indelible mark. I don't have any regrets. I know I did my best.

Tyler Phillips-Banos, caregiver to mom, Wanda

Tyler's professional nursing and corporate healthcare experience runs deep: a Master's in Health Care Administration plus nine years' prior hands-on experience as a Certified Nurse Assistant and a Nurse Clinical Associate II. Despite her lengthy mix of formal credentials, she says "helping persons be the best that they can be" is her true passion. Her contributions to our handbook weigh-in more heavily with practical advice in CAREGIVING, but she also has great perspective on gratitude. Her experience caring for her mother in her own words:

My super-independent Mom worked all our lives—probably too much, as she was a single mom and constantly on the go. My mom and dad owned a mortgage company together before their divorce when I was eight years old. Mom stayed in the mortgage industry for a very long time. Around 2008 when the market crashed, everything went crazy and my mom's life changed. By then I was in my mid-twenties.

Mom wasn't working as much, constantly getting laid off since she was in her mid-50's, so she switched to working temp jobs the next few years. At some point she ended up caring for an elderly woman who was a friend of the family.

That's when my two sisters and I began to notice something wasn't right: Mom would miss freeway exits driving to our homes. She was still living on her own and still driving to help with the grandkids but then she started to literally get lost driving to my house— a place she came so often it should not have been an issue.

The elderly woman mom helped take care of passed away, so the best option seemed to move Mom in with my sister. Soon after, we found a neurologist who diagnosed her with dementia.

My sisters and I were determined to keep her at home as long as we possibly could—honestly, we thought we could keep her at home forever. In retrospect, we only did it for the length we did because there were three of us. It just got crazy sometimes, constantly rotating which two sisters would bump heads while the third would have to mediate.

Now Mom is in a care facility and doing well. It's a small enough place she feels as if it's her home. We all visit often, but it's still difficult to see her sick.

What's To Come

The first "half" of this book begins with the **SELF-CARE** because that's the only way you're going to be prepared to see this new caregiving role physically, mentally, and emotionally through to a positive and successful outcome. To help you navigate the treacherous waters of caregiving, my advice is assembled under four over-arching themes: **CALM, NOURISH, CONNECT** and **SOUND REST.**

Don't let the word "treacherous" scare you, but all of the amazingly strong women interviewed agree that this is hard work. That said, we also agree there is **LOVE** to be had, lots of it—sweetness, laughter and some fun, too. It's about holding onto the good times to balance out the difficult ones. As with all things in life, we may choose to see the glass half-empty or half-full. Caregiving requires healthy perspectives, so while we always try for the latter, that's a tough ask when you're frustrated, angry or just plain exhausted and haven't had any time for yourself. Trust me, all of this will help.

The **CALM** section guides you to tranquility by quieting the mind to stay present; finding your unique daily mantra; and balancing your nervous system through a meditation practice. Above all, you must learn to trust yourself and your instincts. Any time we examine our lives (journeys, paths, whatever you want to name it,) there is an internal knowing and this skill has a name: instinct. You may call it your gut feelings or reactions instead, but they all require learning how to deeply listen to yourself.

Breathing and Releasing helps you stay grounded and remain present through the tough times.

The **NOURISH** section covers exactly what it says, except nourishment comes from more than food. Food's importance is covered, naturally (including my all-time favorite "green juicing" to achieve daily maximum nutrition), but that's only part of the requirements to keep your immune system working at optimum level. Nourishment also means enjoyable activity and restful sleep (including napping) to refresh our bodies and spirits.

Finally, nourishing our spirit is the secret to feeling alive, whole, and ready to take on any challenges caregiving throws our way. That's where Nourishment evolves into Connection...

The **CONNECT** section is about healing. We introduce the power and importance of Nature, conscious movement, such as walking (and my favorite, Yoga.) plus staying grounded. These are all ways to feel connected to ourselves, our parent, and those around us during this uncertain, chaotic, and emotionally draining time. Additionally, we learn to foster Perspective and Gratitude. (Perspective to see the glass as half-full.)

Gratitude helps us understand what we're doing now is part of our life experience, so we better find things to be grateful for in the process. That ability makes it much more rewarding than you can even imagine.

CONNECT means knowing when to disconnect, too: Ways to escape everyday routines and just let the mind be occupied by others' journeys or maybe even learn something new. Reading, journaling, "me time"—it boils down to boundaries, (another topic which comes up more than once in this book.)

Putting even a few of the **CALM, NOURISH & CONNECT** practices into action will alleviate stress, but **SOUND REST** is the most important. And there's a reason: it's profound what the body requires to heal and repair each day's stressors. If everyone slept the full recommended eight hours of nightly sleep most medical professionals recommend, we'd all sleep one third of our lives. Add caregiving into that mix? Sleep becomes the most essential tool to heal and repair before tackling the next day.

These tips will help you in less-obvious ways, too. Remember, things take time and unfortunately, humans aren't that inclined to change. You won't realize benefits from trying something once. In fact, most self-help gurus unanimously proclaim that 21-day repetition is required to make a change stick. Be patient. Give your mind and body a chance to adjust.

"Self-Care is never a selfish act-
it is simply good stewardship of the only gift I have"
-Parker Palmer

Once the **SELF-CARE** foundation is covered, our handbook switches gears to the practical aspects of **CAREGIVING**—the whole reason you're here. You'll find resources to help navigate the waters and understand how to prepare yourself for the ever-changing journey. The information clarifies your role and lets you honor yourself and your parent, while also forgiving yourself for being imperfect. (Yes, self-forgiveness is required in the process of caregiving, for your state of mind and overall well-being.)

But Forgiveness applies to your parent and all the parties you'll encounter along the way, too. Think of it as the act of letting go of everything (including persons) that weigh you down. You become lighter. You can love yourself more—which translates into an improved quality of care you can offer your parent.

Unfortunately, there is no Universal Manual. Learn to trust the process. Each circumstance is as unique as each person's life. In the end, it comes down to trusting your caregiving for mom or dad just as they did when they raised you. Hearing others' stories, struggles, triumphs, and tips should help you feel more comfortable. Just knowing you're not alone and you're on the right path holds tremendous value. I hope you'll also pick up ideas and new insights, too.

I know you're ready: You're here, you're reading this, you're strong. Congratulations for choosing to approach your role with newfound compassion and intention.

PART ONE
FILLING THE WELL:
SELF CARE FIRST

Introducing Self-Care—the newest, hottest, buzzword-of-the-moment. But what does it even mean?

Take care of yourself is something we hear all the time. Is it just a ploy to sell us lotions and potions? Or is this something we need to pay attention to?

I want to emphasize what I refer to as self-care is really SELF-LOVE wrapped into preventative maintenance. Self-care and preventative maintenance might make you think of the big categories such as being a vegan, a runner, or going to the gym every day; however, it's the small, daily things that add up in everyday care. Routines as small as drinking enough water, eating nutrient-dense meals, drinking green juice, getting a good night's sleep, or even just slowing down.

Daily practice of these seemingly small rituals adds up, they accumulate. They build internal dialogue that in turn, builds up our immune systems which prevents us from getting sick. Think about it this way: walk every day, and in a few short weeks you just may find yourself jogging or even running during your walk. It's that simple.

When you practice daily self-care, you are practicing self-love. That's a good— make that GREAT—thing. Follow daily self-care while caregiving, no matter how small. Bodies respond almost immediately to daily self-care.

Pause for a moment to take a deep breath.
Say to yourself, I've got YOU!

> ## A Caregiver's Perspective: Erin
>
> My Dad restored classic cars for a living. He was only 47 when he was first diagnosed with cancer. He was still working every day doing what he loved and had no idea all of this was going on inside him.
>
> Now I'm in my forties, and it's always there, in the back of my mind: *When is something going to happen to me? When is the other shoe going to drop?*

One of the problems with our society is the public mostly relies on doctors to give them health advice. Doctors are essential for when bodies need immediate attention and for annual checkups, (one form of proactive preventative care); but what tends to happen is we neglect ourselves, then an issue inevitably arises, and if it sticks around long enough, that's when we go to a doctor to "solve it" without addressing the patterns that got us into that condition to begin with.

Most doctors rarely impart pre-emptive nutrition and preventative self-care information to their patients (or at least they don't focus on that.) I believe it's because they don't have the time, or perhaps they believe they are only there to assist in fixing problems. Maybe both? (Notice I didn't say all doctors. Some understand that sharing this information is crucial.)

So without prompts to instill preventative self-care routines, we tend to let things go too far. I saw it first hand with my parents: as if dismissing the aches and pains would make the issues go away. Unfortunately, they don't. Issues only get worse. Those issues are our bodies telling us to *pay attention, adjust, get moving*. We need to follow the signs of what needs adjusting. Joints often ache because the body is letting us know it needs *more* movement, or a different type—not less movement. But we subconsciously shut down instead of giving in to 'hear' our instinctual connections. Therefore, learning deep listening becomes an important skill to develop.

Most of us don't know how to self-care, let alone during this emotional time. It's hard when you're always running to make the next appointment; or making sure the right medications are distributed at the right time, and that meals and laundry are getting done, plus personal hygiene is addressed—being there to support *their* emotional rollercoaster... the list goes on. But good caregiving means your parent will have a longer, healthier life.

Self-care and caregiving go hand-in-hand. Give proper care to yourself and in turn to the person under your charge. If you're being unkind to You and Your Body first, it's almost impossible to be kind to another person. (I did specify 'almost.' You might pull it off for brief stints but eventually you will find yourself angry and frustrated all the time, which will likely manifest into your own sickness.) If you're caring for yourself even 75% of the time, you will still experience anger and frustrating moments, but the rest will balance out.

Remember too, that caregiving for a sick parent means you are already beginning to grieve for them, and likely why caregiving tends to have a lot of sadness. Be gentle with yourself. Go slowly when you can. This is a journey that has a beginning and an end. That may sound harsh, yet I dealt with a lot of death in my life and I still didn't think it was ever going to be over with my dad.

The world is messy. Real life is messy. Caregiving isn't any different so be gentle and kind with yourself. This won't last forever.

My goal is to help you unravel the mess and try to make sense of it. Caregiving journeys continue to morph into many shapes and sizes: Some days are a breeze with lightness and laughter; Others feel as if your heart has been pulled out of your chest. Prepare for lots of changes. Pressure builds up and needs release. Crying is normal so give yourself permission to cry (you may be surprised how much it helps.) I did, but this is in my character. When I first met my sweet husband, he would say, "You cry at every movie," and I thought to myself *Oh, just wait...*

Speaking of, I have always been an emotional person. This quality is a blessing for caregivers because it provides an innate level of compassion and empathy that makes one understand another's pain. Every emotion is okay, just keep a check on them, meaning don't allow them to take over for too long to avoid getting so emotional that everything seems bigger to the extent you can't give care, even to yourself. A thick line exists between feeding into emotion too deeply, too often, and completely disregarding them.

As for those who are less expressive and uncomfortable with emotional demonstrations, learn to accept that it's okay to feel overwhelmed at times. Good without bad doesn't exist. Practicing balance versus suppression will keep situations from spiraling. So much of caregiving is about managing our emotional versus our practical inclinations. Take pride that you have the detachment angle down, now allow yourself to *feel*.

Whether you are emotional or stoic, you must reach out for help to keep the other at bay. If you can manage the time and cost, seeing a therapist during this time is a wonderful idea. These days a lot of therapy is available over the phone or video. Besides being a time-saver, it may be easier all-around for scheduling and affordability.

A Caregiver's Perspective: Lexie

I learned the hard way: In order to be a caregiver, you have to have a 'well' and your 'well' needs to be full...

We never imagined Mom was going to live as long as she did, so we weren't prepared for long-term care or long-term goals. About six years in, I thought I was completely losing it. I knew I had to pivot to keep my autonomy or I was going to lose my whole self. I needed to orbit around myself again.

That's when I decided, *when I'm with Mom, I may be in her world, but when I'm not, I need to switch back to me.* That meant enjoying quality time with my husband, my dancing, my surfing... I used yoga to fill myself up. All the things I love to do.

Every thought in my head couldn't be about 'Mom'.... It was swallowing me up.

A Caregiver's Perspective: Val

You do just get thrown into being a caregiver, so you must deal with your own thinking.

It was an honor for me, so it wasn't as hard. Were there challenges? Yes, of course there were. Seeing your loved one deteriorate is hard. It is no fun. How do you process what's happening and separate *"what do I need?"* You're not going to get what you need from the person for whom you're caregiving. You may not get anything from this at all. You just pour what you get right back into them, so what you really need to think about is, *"How do I fill up my gas tank?"*

Get a Post-it or small piece of paper and tape.
Write "Don't forget to breathe. :)"
Now place that on your everyday bathroom mirror.

Visual reminders and notes are a great help when we are overwhelmed.

CALM

Our breathing rhythm provides a sense of normalcy. Look at how we breathe when we are angry, upset, or anxious—we're not even breathing. When your breathing is fast or irregular, re-establish 'rhythm' and you'll just click back into the rhythm of life.
- Dr. Penelope Potter

Be Present

When my dad began frequently falling in his Pennsylvania apartment (also annoying the neighbor below him), our best option to keep him SAFE at the time was his first nursing home. Thankfully, it was very close to home so I could go there every day, even two-to-three times a day, but Dad landed in a negative place, literally and figuratively. That was painful: Dad was unwell and unhappy.

This was a medal-worthy time of frustration of the many stages we experienced together. Frankly, he was depressed, and we felt hopeless. (It was a relief he only stayed there for a few months until we found his second, final home in New York where he was actually happy most of the time.)

Anyway, one day as I left the house to go see him in that first place, for whatever reason I had the idea it may be the last time. As I headed out, I told myself: *Stay present. Listen to his words—really listen. Enjoy all the little things—even if they are frustrating; even if I want to scream because I'm worried about him and the whole situation where he currently lives...*

A Caregiver's Perspective: Susan

Caregivers juggle so many things—we just feel compelled to respond to every demand right away. But when I'm emotional, I feel it in my body. Every person does. You must learn to take care of that because if you don't, it's gonna snowball into something bigger...

When my blood's boiling, I permit myself to pause. I mean, I say that now as I sit here with my cup of coffee, but in hindsight I wish I had done that way more. When you're 'in it,' you can't see it that way. You must give yourself permission to pause when you feel emotional responses starting to brew within your body. Learn to try taking pressure off yourself because everyone just needs a moment to find clarity. It really is the most helpful.

Mantra

The concept of Acceptance is the next place to shift your attention. Change will always be challenging to different degrees depending on your situation, which means that accepting the circumstances you face each day becomes unavoidable. Every little gesture of self-care added to daily routines will help you manage this distress and will have a cumulative effect to ground you and help you feel whole. With all caregiving, little changes you make within your self-care will assist you with learning acceptance. Besides acceptance, caregiving's frenzied energy also requires several more calming practices in your tool belt to help you get grounded. Mantras are a great start. Mantras are phrases or sentences that take your focus back to the Present, back to the Positive. The more we remind ourselves of what we want (or need) to hear, the more we become it. Words give comfort just as photos do. They remind us we are connected which helps us stay calm inside. Think of mantras as the same as having framed photos of friends and family around the house—friendly reminders that we matter and can make a difference in a loved one's life, including our own! Whenever I'm missing Dad, a mantra helps me remember the good times etched in my mind forever.

The beauty of reciting daily mantras is that they may be said anytime, all day long. Face it, regardless of who is on your team or how much support you have, caregiving is difficult at times. Admit it's hard work: It is hard and that's okay. Your own sweet words can help you plow through the many challenges to get to the many tender moments' finish lines (truly just moments and usually fleeting but they provide so much satisfactory richness to counter the tough times.) You may learn to block out the negative, but you will always carry those tender times with you.

So, let's create mantras that you can work with. Let your mantras be personal. Make the words relate to what you're doing, or where you are mentally and emotionally at this moment, such as, "My Mom is love and I am love" or "We've got this." Or something simple that just says *"I am Strong"* or *"I am okay"*. Perhaps try generating from your personal spiritual practice or worship traditions? Whether a single word, a phrase, or even a sound or visual – mantras work.

* * *

My personal mantra during my caregiving years was *"I love you,"* and it applied two ways:

- saying it to myself because I needed to hear it;
- and saying it to Dad because I knew he did, too.

Whenever I faced challenging times, I found myself saying over and over again, *I love you. I love you. I love you!*

If that doesn't resonate, what works for **YOU**? You won't use it unless you feel it, so really try to pinpoint what you like to hear... *need* to hear. Tap into that intuition because remember, giving to your parent is truly giving back to yourself. Try a few out to see what works before committing to one for the time being. Just make it personal and something that feels right in your body when you repeat it. Keep in mind: don't choose just one for the long haul! Have several and rotate or change them to fit your shifting dynamics, even daily if you wish.

Ideas for Mantras:

Use the phrase "I am" to start.
They are powerful words that help you maintain power.

*I am:*_____
Strong, Love, Worthy, Giving, Present,
Giving Service, Strength, Resilience, Acceptance...

Repeat your mantra with your eyes closed 1-3 minutes a day. You may be seated, lying down--anywhere you are comfortable.

In addition, I keep a list of things to remember on my mirror and it really supports me in my daily life. Make other 'mantra notes' such as I am *STRONG* or I am *LOVING* to hang around the house, especially on mirrors.

Meditation

A Caregiver's Perspective: Penelope

Other than the love for my mother—that was the main thing, of course—one word that got me through: Meditation. I was able to meditate often as Mom did a lot of sleeping. Thankfully, it wasn't as if I had to prepare meals for her every day, so that made things easier, too.

No other way around it, in terms of taking care of myself—my own mind and emotions—being able to go into that quiet, peaceful place of light and love. I'd been meditating for ten years by that point, so it was the meditation that saved me.

Caregiving pulls us in many different directions at once and requires us to constantly check boxes and get things done. This non-stop pressure creates a kind of stress that puts individuals in "auto-pilot" mode. Sound familiar?

Meditation is an amazing tool to quiet the mind from that daily chatter.

I used to think one could only meditate sitting on a yoga mat in complete silence, back perfectly aligned, eyes closed…

I was wrong.

Now I always hear others complain: *"I can't meditate" "It's too hard," "My mind just keeps racing and so many thoughts pop into my head."*

I understand all of this, and yes, thoughts will come and go; but the idea is to watch those thoughts as if they are clouds moving across the sky. Over time those thoughts calm down. Don't assume your thoughts will disappear. Sure, perhaps after time with a dedicated meditation practice. How long, you ask? No one knows an exact answer as we are all different. Meditation is a practice and the more you practice, the more your mind recognizes the practice. Eventually your body and mind will come to expect meditation and you will crave it.

So, NOW is the time start. Whenever we wait for everything to be *perfect*, we find excuses to stall. Simply start slowly and it will inevitably become just as brushing your teeth. Why not incorporate it into your morning routine, right before or after brushing your teeth?

When you're just starting, having someone guide you is the easiest way to get still and glide right into the process. I highly recommend trying the resources of master meditation leader and teacher, davidji. His website, **davidji.com**, provides guided meditations that I found to be most helpful during my caregiving years. I'd lie on my bed, give myself permission for some 'me time', and then randomly pick one (10-30) minute session to listen to which always seemed to be exactly what I needed to hear. I found davidji's voice so soothing, I'd be transformed and transported to another place almost instantly.

Meditation is an incredible way to let go. Regardless of where you're at in your practice or budget, meditation is a popular topic of online searches covering all kinds of guides and audio styles. Try a variety to find formats that suit your taste, then download various recording lengths right onto your phone so they're handy when you need them without requiring an internet connection. (If you're on a budget, most resources offer free guided options, too.) The convenience of pre-recorded sessions checks one more thing off your To-Do list that you don't have to oversee. I am forever grateful for those Heaven-sent guided meditations.

Recommendation:
Meditate a minimum of two minutes a day.

- ✦ Set a timer for two minutes.
- ✦ Sit in a chair, or lie down on a mat on the floor, sofa or bed, whatever is available, so you don't have an excuse to skip it.
- ✦ Close your eyes.
- ✦ Be in silence; or, Repeat "OHM" or your Mantra silently to yourself.

See MANTRA, prior section.

If two minutes is easy, try three...
Work your way up until you can comfortably sit until you feel you're done, however long that becomes.
No need for judgement. What works for you?
If two minutes feels long, try one minute. The important thing is to just do it.

A Caregiver's Perspective: Amber

As a caregiver, you always hear "take care of yourself," but it's really very hard to take care of yourself because you're now the brain for *two*: yourself and the person you're responsible for. To a degree you even take on their emotions because you're trying to fill in: If they're having a good day, you want to make this their best day ever, even if you don't feel that yourself. And of course when they're sad, you're sad, even if you started out upbeat and motivated.

Journal

Writing in a journal is another great way to unwind. This is especially effective if your mind is always racing with To-Do lists. (The To-Do's always seem long, especially as shopping, errands, and doctor appointments pile up.) Journaling my To-Do lists really worked when I was caregiving for Dad. Now I still make my To-Do list the night before so my mind can rest, especially when I have a photo or video shoot the next day.

So, whether it's a list of errands and reminders, or simply your way of recording and processing the day's events and emotions, write it all down and get it off your chest.

A Caregiver's Perspective: Amber

I often do not feel as though I'm keeping it together but crying and writing in my journal are the two biggest things that help. Those have been working for me for a long time.

First, caregivers must cry. One night, I was up at 2 a.m. feeling overwhelmed and sad watching Mom slip away from me in real-time so, I let the tears flow. It's really scary, so just let it flow...

I also keep a journal to document everything and use this as a release. Documenting is very important because you usually feel bombarded. When my dad died of prostate cancer, we had months to prepare. In the end he had pain, but medicine kept him out for 3-4 hours at a time. Then eventually he was gone...

Mom is very different, ever-changing. Finding some routine or schedule is challenging. I document what's going on so I'm able to provide specifics of the shifting information to anyone else that's caring for her. If you don't, it's as if you're trying to manage all of it while going down a black hole.

A Caregiver's Perspective: Lexie

I always carried a notebook around for all the things that would come up. Instead of trying to keep track of it all in my brain, I would just write it down. Even simple reminders such as "Next trip to see Mom, don't forget _____."

Tip:
Buy 2 journals. One to carry with you and another to have by your bed.
Keeping a journal by your bed is a great way to dump all the caregiving stressors of the day.

Trust Yourself

(Or, How I Learned Self-Trust Through Caregiving Early-On...)

I now know there was a reason for my innate nurturing skills: I was born a natural caregiver. My mother, Barbara, was an ill woman. She had rheumatic fever as a child which affected her heart, which in turn affected her daily health into adulthood. Additionally, she was plagued with a tremendous amount of anxiety and depression. She was diagnosed with schizophrenia later in life. As a child I was responsible for her caregiving.

Caregiving is a lot to ask of a child, but it was my duty, and I didn't know anything else. I was expected to take charge, and that's exactly what I did. When I talk about being 'in charge', what I am really saying is overseeing the daily happenings for our family: food, cleaning, menial tasks.

Looking back, what I mostly did was self-care. When a parent is absent, the child needs to take control. I helped Mom any way I could when Dad was working (laundry, cooking, cleaning, my brother), but the skills I learned back then have remained, such as self-talk. I developed a self-talk where I'd look in the mirror and tell myself "*You are okay. You've got this,*"—but in a way a child speaks to herself. I don't remember my exact words, but I do recall the way I spoke: with care, concern, love and empathy.

I am grateful for the discovery of self-talk back then. At times it saved me from feeling lonely and afraid. This is something we all need to do. If a mirror helps, use one. My mirror was attached to my vanity, (actually three mirrors so I never felt alone, which may sound strange, but it was my reality.)

Fast forward from childhood to adulthood, and that self-talk kicked into high gear while I managed both parents' declining health, (Dad after Mom.) I was by my mother's side when the doctor diagnosed her with ovarian cancer and told her she had six months to live. I did the best I could taking her to all her chemo appointments and helping out around their house while she went through cancer treatments. It was the first time I played the caregiving role as a grown woman. It brought back memories, but it also prepared me for caregiving to my dad later in life. My dear mother, Barbara, passed away six months later at the age of 57. I was devastated. I was around 30 years old and didn't have the grounding I do now.

Almost 15 years later, once again I was with Dad at his doctor appointment when we heard the news, he had been diagnosed with lymphoma cancer. I was beside myself. Both of us were so shaken by the diagnosis, we drove home in complete and utter silence. There was no self-talk; I could hardly drive. Time lasted forever in that silent car. No words could comfort us—a numbing experience to say the least.

A few days later once the shock wore off, I told myself I would do whatever it took to make sure Dad went through all of it as painlessly as possible. This time, I was 44 and had the emotional, physical, and spiritual tools to understand and handle the ins and outs of what was needed. I could help him maintain a good life for as long as he lasted. I made a commitment from that moment and stuck to it, no matter what.

Still, I struggled with depression, anxiety, and loneliness at times, often feeling I didn't have the strength required to manage it all. In addition to caregiving for Dad, I was running a successful photography business and household with my business partner/husband. Balancing it all was a juggling act. The mantras and self-talk kicked into high gear—any encouragement to keep me motivated and on track.

So much caregiving is based on instinct. Go with your instinct—chances are you're doing it right. However, if you're having doubts, push the pause button on self-talk. Even though I've been a caregiver my whole life, I'll admit that not raising children sometimes felt as if I might have been missing some skillset I should have known about, e.g., *Am I doing this right*? If you're self-doubting, reach out to a friend, family member, neighbor, heck, even a stranger—anyone that can reinforce self-trust and confidence with your decisions. I'd strike up a conversation with the person at the farmers market selling me peaches, just to let off steam or get advice. You'd be surprised how people want to help and how many have gone through similar situations.

Believe me, I understand how hard this work is; and while I can't take away the burden you're bearing, or the confusion and suffering you may feel, I can help you remember that we are only given what we can handle in Life.

You are Strong.
You've got this.
Now let's go!

Don't forget to take deep breaths.
Let's do that now, together:

- Take a deep breath through your nose, keeping your mouth closed.
- Slowly count to three... 1... 2... 3...
- (No need to rush.)
- Now let it out slowly thru your mouth.

Breath will be your guide. It is **always** there for you.

A Caregiver's Perspective: Amber

The best piece of advice is to be 'in the moment' in all aspects. At first I had to have all the answers: *What stage is she in? What exactly do I need to be doing right now?*...

Sometimes when you're in Caregiving Mode and so hard and fast to the rules, you miss the sweet moments. For example, she'd be sleeping, and I'd get anxious because, "Oh, I need to give her that medicine now!"

Instead, you learn which tasks are not so time-sensitive. Whenever you get extra time, take that for yourself. Ask yourself: *What do I need right now?* Then do whatever comes in. Talk yourself through all options. Maybe nap, or read that article, or get some exercise...

So yes, while you need to plan, remember to stay in the moment and trust yourself or you'll make yourself crazy.

NOURISH

A Caregiver's Perspective: Val

It was my pleasure and my honor to give care to my mother, but what I didn't do was give care to myself. Since my daughter and I ride horses, we have to be strong. You must be in shape to ride a horse, especially English (a riding style.) I used to be a gym fanatic working out six days a week, but I wasn't going to the gym anymore. Plus, I took on all the responsibility of the family business managing rental properties.

I do physical work for all the properties, working alongside the plumbers and the electricians, as well as other skills my dad taught me on the job. However, I just didn't take care of myself during that period. I gained weight, going from a size 6 to a size 14. My blood pressure went way up: usually 110/70, it spiked up in the 200's. My doctor warned me I was at risk for a stroke.

It's been only a year since my mom passed and I'm still recovering and working on myself, the healthy self I used to be.

Nutrition

The term Health 'Nut' is funny. It implies that because someone cares about themselves and their health, well, they're *nutty*. As if something is wrong with them?

This can't be further from the truth. Believe the opposite: intentional focus on your health is the sanest thing you can do for yourself.

Now, I admit I am a Health NUT! But it was a process. I'm sharing a bit of my journey into health starting with Nutrition and ending with Sleeping as the core tenets of Self-Care as the information may help you on your own journey.

I came from an extended Italian American family during the 1970's when the *get-it-quick* mentality was on the rise. Packaged foods were popping up everywhere: Pop-Tarts, instant breakfast drinks, processed cheese spreads, and so on. The movement away from whole foods might have been the general beginning of what was making people sick, but it definitely made for a lot of sick individuals in my immediate family view (Mom included.) In the 70's, the average person didn't quite understand the ramifications of what we were doing to ourselves. Lack of nutritional foods, high stress, and smoking all contributed, (again, at least in my family.)

In high school I decided to give up things that were bad for me. For some reason, my intuition red-flagged fast foods and packaged foods, so I started to take the healthy route, which wasn't easy at first. I didn't understand nutrition at all, so I ate a a ton of salads plus a lot of dairy products: cheese and all kinds of yogurts filled with sugar. I also didn't know where to turn for answers, so I started taking vitamins thinking that was the answer to what we all needed more of. I overdid it, with iron pills especially.

I didn't realize I was overdoing it until the day I had such bad stomach cramps my mother had to take me to the doctor who then promptly informed us that if I continued taking that many iron pills, I could die. Pretty serious stuff. Obviously, I had no clue what nutrition was all about! But I knew I didn't want to grow old and be sick in bed. I just didn't know anyone to talk to about health.

So, I looked to health magazines. Now this was over thirty years ago, and salads seemed to be the only thing all magazines agreed on and recommended for a healthy body, along with various exercise regiments. Lucky for me, I liked salads and vegetables in general, and I also enjoyed exercising so I looked for routines that I could follow in my bedroom.

It turns out spinach was my favorite food, (maybe watching too many Popeye cartoons on television as a kid—who knows?) So, my diet basically came to consist of lots of pasta, bread, cheese pizza, and more cheese (Italian, remember?) Then salads and spinach and more spinach.

Green Juice

Fast-forward 10 years: I had moved to Seattle with Charlie, (my then-boyfriend-now-husband.) One day we were shopping downtown looking at appliances when we saw a juicer on sale. *Great!* we thought. *We will get one to make fresh orange juice for our Sunday brunch gatherings!*

Sure enough, we made lots of fresh-squeezed orange juice with that first juicer. We drank *so much* fresh orange juice and not just for brunch gatherings. It was just so delicious. That is, until Charlie's ankles broke out in hives. Turns out, my husband had an allergic reaction to the amount of citrus we were digesting. (Being acidic, too much citrus goes against the grain of what bodies really want.) Needless to say, the hives kiboshed our freshly-squeezed orange juice indulgences, but this was ultimately a good discovery because it started us on a new path in our health journey. Nowadays, we don't avoid all acidic foods, but we balance how much we consume.

Shortly after that phase, I came upon the book *Juicing for Life*. (Calbom and Keane. Avery Publishing Group: 1992.) This book was practically glowing on the shelf, screaming, *pick me up!* So of course I thumbed through and promptly bought it.

This book literally changed our lives. It was incredible health insight in just one book. We absolutely devoured all the information pertaining to healthy habits and curing ailments through juicing. It contains recipes for every kind of juice concoction and describes the health benefits of each, for example: Need better sleep? Drink celery juice in the evening as it calms your nervous system. Feel a cold coming on? Add ginger.

Once we put it to use, we started to understand our bodies in a more whole form and began juicing green juice, carrot juice, or mixtures of healthy juices depending how we felt each week, even each day. I'll admit we favored carrots at the start. At that point our fridge was filled with 25 pounds of carrots a week. We drank so much carrot juice at the start that the palms of my hands and feet turned orange. Seattle friends always wondered why I was tan. People would ask, "Did you just get back from vacation in Hawaii?"

"Oh, no," I would say. "I drink Carrot juice!"

(If you are familiar with Seattle, winters get dark. It is not unusual for the sun to remain out of view for three weeks at a time so, let's just say no one is getting tan during Seattle winters.)
Obviously, this wasn't a balanced juicing routine quite yet. We

were still learning and experimenting, but all setbacks were eye-opening awakenings into improving our health and habits.

Consuming more greens in your life is key—in fact, the biggest NOURISHMENT tip that I swear by. Getting enough nutrients in general is difficult enough. It becomes an outright task while caregiving, mostly because of time constraints. And since we can't possibly get all the recommended greens into our body by eating them alone, green juicing is the answer. It absolutely works for me. One of the many reasons I adopted drinking green juice is that it provides loads of nutrients in a simple drink. It really helps when time is an issue, (which is almost always.)

Attention to my own nutrition consumption has been a life saver for my nervous system, overall health and well-being. After all, a strong body goes hand-in-hand with a strong mind (or quiet one, whichever way you look at it.) Over the next ten years I adopted even more healthy routines, all the while a yoga student with a steady practice (since age 18, but more on that later.)

This is hard stuff. Stop and breathe.
Seek support. Ask for help.
You've got this!

All our circumstances are unique, so please be kind to yourself as you adjust your dietary habits to better support optimum health. Keep in mind bodies take time to adjust, so start slowly with small amounts and work up. It will probably be one of the harder things to modify because eating habits become so ingrained. We are all different and each body has individual requirements, so of course, listen to your own body and always check with a health professional to make sure any new dietary adjustment works for you; but when done correctly, green juicing's benefits should outweigh any objections.

Hydrate

I'm a water drinker who has learned most people are not. Drinking eight glasses of water a day clears our heads and makes us feel better overall, again, both of which make us better caregivers.

I started to understand hydration needs once I moved to Southern California. A yoga teacher asked me "Are you drinking enough water?" And that's when I realized I was thirsty. Get in the habit of drinking water before you get to the point of feeling thirsty. And Summers outdoors aren't the only time we lack hydration; one may be dehydrated just as easily during Winter months indoors with the heat on as well.

Years ago, when I didn't drink a lot of water I got frequent headaches. I have since learned that a headache may be a sign to drink more water. Since then, I always have water on my desk, in my car, and bring it to meetings when appropriate.

For those of you saying, *but I don't like water*, try adding fruit: lemon, lime, orange, strawberries, kiwi, peach—any citrus or fruit you might think of. There are flavored electrolyte powders you can add to water, too.

And while you're at it, please check that your parent is getting enough water. Older folks have problems with dehydration and, from what I understand, it causes or exacerbates many ailments. One for sure is UTI's. Share this with your mom or dad and make sure they are getting their water as well. Let's all drink up!

> **Tip:**
> Get multiple portable water bottles so you always have water with you.

A Caregiver's Perspective: Susan

I will be honest with you: Self-care was a challenge for me. My self-care really started after my mother passed— or maybe *right* before, when I finally realized I needed to have a different relationship with food.

The most self-care I granted myself was a cabin stay, therapy, and support from friends. Otherwise, I was medicating myself with food and booze throughout.

I tried to exercise, but I got very heavy during that whole time—the heaviest I have ever been in my life. No surprise because it was such a hard, hard time.

So I would say don't be hard on yourself and do the best you can.

Alcohol

A Caregiver's Perspective: Lexie

Whenever I had a lot of crises with my dad, say an entire month (which happened,) I remember going out a few times that year and getting a bottle of wine and drinking it on the back porch until I passed out.

Drinking alcohol is one of the things individuals tend to do when they are in crisis mode, so after that, whenever I thought about buying a bottle of wine, I knew right then that I was feeling ungrounded.

Later on, after being with my mom for three days, I'd go to the ocean instead and just watch the waves for 10 minutes to get grounded before I went home. It let the days melt away so I wouldn't bring stress home with me.

Sometimes we think a drink is what we need to alleviate stress, especially when caregiving. Remember, alcohol is a depressant. There's a fine line when you're already feeling vulnerable and emotional. It may trigger a slight depression as opposed to helping you feel better. Try as best you can to limit or avoid drinking during this time.

Don't give up; this doesn't last forever.
There is a sweetness in your act of caregiving.
Witness and look for the nectar.

CONNECT

Connection is an important pillar of self-care during this uncertain, chaotic, and emotionally draining time. The following section explores ways to connect to ourselves, our parent, and those around us. As with everything in life, there are two sides: sometimes the most healing is sharing time with another; other times it is disengaging and reconnecting with ourselves. All of the following may be adjusted to accommodate social or solo activity.

Nature Heals

A Caregiver's Perspective: Susan

My Mother was in an assisted living facility in a rural area near my brother, and since the hotels there were terrible, I decided to rent a cabin at a nearby river. It was a Godsend. Even If I was gone all day, coming back to that place was magical. It really was so relaxing to wake up there. That kept me sane during the most stressful, painful period of my life. Nature was the answer I didn't know I needed – the outdoors: plants and animals, the land, bodies of water, the air, the sky...

Having a comfortable place to stay where I had privacy was very important to me. There was a little stream that went by the cabin that reminded me of a song I sang in a New York choir I belonged to. It was about the river that keeps rolling along. So, every day I would see that water moving along a little differently: some days it would be low, some days high; but the water just kept moving... it just kept coming.

I found caregiving to be a very depleting act. Nature refueled me. In turn, I was able to give more. Life goes on, life continues. These gentle reminders from nature were very soothing.

There were millions of 'lightning bugs' at night. I would just fix myself a cocktail and sit out on the deck and wait for the 'lightning bug' show. The 'lightning bugs' were fantastic: being in touch with nature, connecting to my senses which connected me to my childhood summers in my grandmother's big yard with my mom and brother. It brought back memories when we'd catch 'lightning bugs', which for me, are very symbolic of good times, innocent times, and sweetness.

Those 'lightening bugs' at the cabin were just magic— as if the stars came down from the heavens to float above the grass. What a juxtaposition from NYC. That was comforting.

If you can, find a place of respite. It really nurtures you while you are caregiving. Mine reminded me to slow down and take a breath. It was totally worth it.

Movement Heals

Yoga, walking, hiking, biking, jump roping, spinning, rowing, treadmill, dancing in the kitchen... whatever you do, Get Moving. Your day will go so much smoother. With a little movement, you will have more energy and find more ease in daily life. Just ten minutes to an hour a day keeps your mood regulated and your spirits lifted. Use whatever you've got.

Yoga and walking are my daily practices. Combining yoga and walking with meditation will manage your stress. I know that's a lot to digest when you're caregiving, but movement makes or breaks your mental health, so try and schedule activity into every day.

When I was caregiving for Dad, we lived near a river, so I would walk down to the river to get some silence whenever I was able to get myself there. The peace really helped me connect to the water and sometimes just turn off and stare off into space.

It's wonderful if you have a pretty cabin by a river or other place to enjoy, but Nature doesn't have to be a grand study of rural wildlife. It may be as simple as observing the plants and trees that grow in your area or your neighbor's backyard. In a city, it might be a walk in a park listening to the birds or observing the habits of squirrels.

A Caregiver's Perspective: Tyler

I really became aware of gratitude when I was working with kids with cancer. Imagine a kid that wants to go outside and play but can't because they can't walk, or they are on radiation and can't leave their room, or they are nauseated that day and can't physically get out of bed...

I thought to myself, *look at me complaining that I don't want to get up and go work out. Now I ask myself, why am I denying myself?* —because maybe one day, I won't be able to. Ever since that shift, I do boot camp and work out four days a week.

Walking to Manage Stress

In my teenage years, I was a caregiver for a baby named Kate. Kate's mom made me promise that if it wasn't raining too hard, I would take the baby out for some fresh air every day after school. I still follow her advice. I find walking to be one of the best habits to manage stress. It's one activity I can't live without. Besides, it's something you can do anywhere, anytime. You only need comfortable shoes such as good sneakers. (I always opt for running shoes. They're most comfortable for my feet and sometimes transitioning into light jogging between walking.) I have two pair, so I don't wear the same ones every day—apparently switching between shoes is better for your posture.

Speaking of good posture, good walking posture is essential. Try to keep yourself upright when walking, that is, don't lean forward too much or you may start having lower back problems. I would go for walks while waiting for my dad at his doctor appointments, especially if they were at the hospital. I'd just cruise around the hospital floor, taking laps. I did the same at his nursing home while Dad was napping. I tried to get steps in whenever I could, since my schedule was so packed between our two lives.

Set out to go outside every day. Mark your calendar to walk a minimum of 30-60 minutes daily. If you skip a day here or there, that is okay, but even walking around the block once will help. If that's not possible, then just get some outdoor air. Breathe in and out slowly for 2 minutes. Don't stop in winter. Bundle up and get some fresh air. Up your game: walk slowly and intentionally. It promotes better health and better sleep, especially during this time.

One important detail if possible: train yourself to walk every day at the same time. This way, once you put on your walking shoes and head out the door, your mind and body know what to expect. Sounds crazy, but it works. For example, I don't enjoy walking in bright sun. I prefer to walk at the end of the day. During winter months, I leave the house at 4:00 p.m. for 1-1.5 hours. In spring and summer, I leave later in the day. Try out a few different times and see what works for you. Carry water and sometimes a hat for shade in summer or warmth in winter.

Once you establish your walk routine, notice all the things around you: look at nature's wonders such as flowers. No flowers? Hear the birds, the leaves rustling on a tree, or study the tree bark. What's happening with the sky today? Are there clouds? Is the sky blue? Noticing what is going on around you is a great way to relax your mind and experience a moving meditation.

A Caregiver's Perspective: Erin

The best form of self-care for me was loving something else. Having a puppy was one of the greatest and biggest gifts—I could get kisses and roll on the floor with this sweet little puppy that needed me—especially if something really difficult happened with my Dad and I didn't want to cry in front of him. I'd take that puppy for a walk around the block and say ten things I was grateful for and really focus on the good. You get lost in it, right? It really helped shift my attitude.

Walking dogs also connected me to my dad in another way. For years, both my parents were volunteers at the Humane society—something I continue to do that makes it even more special. My dad used to say, "When you're feeling helpless, get helpful." So that's what I try to do. It's in my blood to be an animal lover and to be of service volunteering and looking after puppies.

As part of my own recovery time, I walk dogs in the desert. It feels great to get out of my head and stop worrying about the world's problems. There is something so special about being out in the desert sun connecting with these sweet pups—they're just so innocent. It's as good for them as it is for me. So simple: life in its simplest form.

Yoga

A Caregiver's Perspective: Erin

I wish I knew about Yoga when I was going through this, because using my breath and sitting still would have really helped me. It helps get out of *fight* or *flight* mode and into the parasympathetic nervous system*—which I don't think I accessed all those years.

Editor Note: The sympathetic nervous system prepares the body for action and stress, (fight or flight,) while the parasympathetic nervous system restores the body's normal automatic functions to conserve energy (breathing, heart rate, and so forth).

At first, I struggled whether to include Yoga in the Nourishment or Movement sections because it helps achieve balance in both areas. It nourishes us *and* it requires movement. I don't think I could have been so successful throughout the years of caregiving for Dad if I hadn't practiced yoga. (Having gained perspective, I now say 'successful' as it is behind me in the rearview mirror. I was successful caring for him and myself in that I kept it together and avoided getting sick in the process. That's what I call success.)

Anyway, Yoga has been used for over 2000 years in India to heal people from diseases and illness. *Yoga Journal* says, "yoga helps lower stress hormones that compromise the immune system, while also conditioning the lungs and respiratory tract, stimulating the lymphatic system to oust toxins from the body, and bringing oxygenated blood to various organs to ensure their optimal function." Purists describe yoga as the "yoking of the mind and body" meaning it connects our mind and body in a profound way we can't see yet is beneficial in managing stress levels and strengthening the immune system. Yoga requires instinct, trust and paying attention to our breath. Yoga and breathing go hand-in-hand. Every time we practice yoga, we alleviate damaging stress through our breath work. (There is a good reason breathing comes up so much in self-care.)

Yoga is another cumulative act. The more you practice, the less stress you bear and the richer an experience it becomes. The first thing I often hear when I mention yoga is "Oh, I'm inflexible, so I can't do yoga." But yoga is for *everybody*, no matter where your body is in terms of flexibility, strength, weight... yoga IS for you, so do what you can. Besides leaving you feeling grounded and calm, you may be surprised at what comes up for you emotionally. Emotions may come in the form of crying or laughing, both helpful with letting go. (I often experience both, sometimes simultaneously.) Go with your emotions and let them flow. Breathe.

I had the opportunity to study yoga for six years at the Iyengar Institute in New York City, attending classes 3-6 times a week. Most of the teachers studied back in India with yogi Iyengar, himself, while he was still alive, and took yoga postures very seriously but always found humor in every class. With so many different styles of yoga out there, your practice may be informal and still be effective. Find a yoga studio near you. If you're new to yoga, ask whether they have a *gentle*, *beginner*, or *restorative* class to attend, then try incorporating a restorative class once a week during caregiving. Your nervous system will reap the benefits.

I love a restorative class: it requires very little movement. The teacher guides you into a relaxing position on the floor with the help of pillows, bolsters, sometimes blocks and a blanket. You remain in each posture for 2 minutes. You may leave class feeling lethargic, but you generally have a deep sleep that night and the benefits continue to unfold over the next few days, ultimately leaving you feeling delightfully relaxed. (Drink a lot of water after each session to keep those muscles and organs hydrated.)

If a studio or in-person classes aren't convenient (or in the budget,) access classes on your phone or computer. There are free classes throughout social media, or standalone yoga sites. Monthly subscriptions also can be had at very low cost. The only real equipment you need is a non-slip mat or surface. Many teachers provide tips to improvise using household items in place of specialized add-ons.

Chair Movement
If you're unable to leave your parent's side or experiencing your own mobility issues (or just don't want to leave your chair), try *chair yoga* or *chair movement* which are simple exercises you can do in your chair.

No matter what position you're starting in, breathing exercises are essential to warm up:

- ✦ Start by closing your eyes,
- ✦ Breathe in through your nose to a count of 3.
- ✦ Breathe out slowly to a count of 3.
- ✦ Repeat for 3 rounds, then open your eyes slowly.

Chair Armlifts
Sit firmly with your feet on the ground and lift your arms up over head touching your hands. Slowly bring your hands down. Repeat 3 -5 times.

Chair Head Hang

(This one is a good practice once you've already had your coffee intake for the day. Putting your head below your heart grants an energy boost accompanied by a sense of calm.)

Sit firmly with your feet on the ground. Spread your legs hip-width and lean over your chair with your head down. (Don't force anything, just relax and let your head go.) Stay this way for as long as feels comfortable: 30 seconds up to a minute when your body adjusts. Notice the back of the neck, your back, your shoulders releasing... Come up very slowly. Remain seated for several minutes before you stand up.

There are many other options you can do from a chair such as:

- ✦ Purchase 3 lb weights and do mini arm curls towards your chest.
- ✦ Bring your arms out to a T and make a curl with your arms toward your shoulders.
- ✦ Google "chair exercises" for more ideas or look up videos on YouTube.

Movement is the name of the game, so it's important to move a little every day. It's good for Mom or Dad, too, depending on their stage of mobility.

Stop and breathe.
I've got you... You've got this.
You are Stronger than you think you are.
And you are loved.

Reading

OK, so far, we've explored different ways to connect mostly through the body and physical senses, but reading offers mental and emotional reprieve from our own reality by helping us connect to worlds outside our own. Whether we escape into fiction or learn about non-fiction subjects or people separate from ourselves, reading buys our mind a break.

I always found reading an enjoyable way to pass time. I did most of my reading in doctor office lobbies, (so much waiting, so many magazines.) I went through phases of carrying a book in my bag when I knew it was going to be a long day, such as Dad's chemo appointments which lasted anywhere from 8-10 hours. On those days a good book definitely came in handy.

Self-help books are my thing but reading provides a wonderful break whatever your preference of genre or subject matter. All our handbook caregivers agree that reading really helped take their mind away from worries and allowed them some escape.

A Caregiver's Perspective: Val

I love to read. Reading definitely helps me. I'm looking for knowledge on how to advance myself. It helps take my mind off of what's in front of me, so back then it was important, so I wasn't only "caregiving for Mom" all of the time.

I read paperback books so I can write in them. Whatever book I'm reading, I can go back to each page and see my thoughts at the time. We all still have to dream. We need something to look forward to. That's important, otherwise we die inside.

A Caregiver's Perspective: Erin

With my dad and me being so ill at the same time after my accident, we couldn't go anywhere. My reality got kind of small and grim, so reading became a great form of self-care because it was escapism: getting lost in a book outside my wheelhouse such as romance, fantasy, or biographies of historical leaders.

I also read out loud to Dad once his vision went. It was another way we could connect.

Friends

Support is more important than usual during this time in your life: Knowing humans are there for you, even if you don't see them that often or they live in another state. Knowing that you are loved by others in the world that "have your back." There's just something comforting knowing you have options should you need to run an idea by someone or just talk.

In the beginning stages of caregiving, it's hard to understand just how deep into your parent's life you're going to be. How could you? It's new territory. So, in turn, we don't know what to tell our friends. Sometimes when I tried reaching out to distant friends during different stages, I didn't know what to say. One (former) friend even said to me, "You're complaining too much. Where's the Debra I know?"

Okay, NOT the friend I needed at the time but that's okay. People who are unable to accept the stage you're in won't be there for you. Try to be okay with them, then find the ones that will. And try to remain open-minded: some friendships may come back around later, after your caregiving role is complete. Remember, everyone is going through their own journey with their own lessons and experiences. If they had forced time for you now, it probably wouldn't have been the kind that benefitted you, anyway.

While it turned out I only had a couple of friends that I could really call at any given time, what I discovered I really needed was just to know that when all was said and done, I was not alone.

My advice? Let your friends know early in this adventure that you may need their help and ask if they are willing. Find your own words of course, but the idea is to determine who will be there for you.

When you do find the right friend(s), set aside specific time to spend with them. Schedule a date once a week to meet up, especially with those friends, groups, or family members who are good listeners and will help you relax and unwind.

(I can hear you right now, *How am I going to find time to do that?*)

We talk about delegating responsibilities a little later in Caregiving, but it's a great way to start. Please find some support, even one friend, neighbor, or a family member that can help you navigate this challenging time. Someone who can sit with your parent or check in on them during that hour or two a week you get to connect with those outside your caregiving realm. It will make a world of difference in your life.

A Caregiver's Perspective: Erin

Friends were supportive but I did push individuals away. I was so drained. You're grieving while you're caregiving: crying yourself to sleep at night, unsure what's going to happen next. The best friends were those that just reached out and said "I just want you to know I am here for you. You don't have to do anything."

Gratitude & Perspective

Being grateful is hard when you have so much on your shoulders trying to keep it all together, trying to manage your own life alongside your parent's life. I understand because I have been there. None of us sign up for this, so while you're still lying in your bed, before you brush your teeth, meditate, or say your mantras, think about one or two things you're grateful for every morning. They don't need to be big. You don't need to share them with anyone. They are simply for you, your consciousness, and your inner voice to start your day on a positive note.

Say it as a simple affirmation acknowledging your unique perspective. "I am grateful... *for my hot coffee, or the sun is shining, or that I have a warm house to wake up to...*" Its simplicity becomes a profound way to set up a successful day of caregiving.

The last few years of his life, my bedbound dad would say, "I am just grateful I woke up today."
Every time he said it, I paused. It struck me hard. I thought to myself, *now THAT'S powerful gratitude*.

Being grateful just for being alive really puts things in perspective.

A Caregiver's Perspective: Lexie

Sometimes Mom would ask me the same question over and over again (part of her dementia.) Since I didn't want her to feel abandoned, I would briefly leave the room to practice this little gratitude thing to re-group: I'd say all the things that I loved about her and then I would go back in the room and give her a kiss.

A Caregiver's Perspective: Val

One day I listened to my mom recite her wishes to me: "Valerie, I want you to know where (this) is and I want you to know where (that) is..." She continued through her list but then she said, "Now I just thank God that I'm able to remember now so that you know where things are when I'm gone..."

Oh boy, I couldn't keep it together after that.

When I finally got a grip on myself, I walked over, clutched her and said, "Mom, you said you weren't going to leave me."

She calmly replied, "Now Valerie, everyone has to leave." Then she took both of my hands and kissed them and told me, "Thank you for everything."

I took her hands and did the same thing in return telling her, "Thank YOU for everything!"

You've got this.
You are always stronger than you think you are.
I repeat,
YOU ARE STRONGER THAN YOU THINK
you are!

Sound Rest

Sleep

The importance of sleep is well, EVERYTHING: Vital for how we function on any given caregiving day, and vital to stave off the long-term health setbacks of sleep-deprivation.

There is no shortage of research to back this up. Arianna Huffington has written two books on the subject: Thrive and The Sleep Revolution: Transforming Your Life One Night at a Time, the latter of which is a deep dive into the science behind getting a good night's rest. And according to the National Library of Medicine/ National Institutes of Health, studies prove that getting enough sleep is important to our health. [Source: ncbi.nlm.nih.gov]. Even the National Heart, Lung, and Blood Institute agree that people with sleep deficiency have a greater risk of many health complications, including heart disease, kidney disease, high blood pressure, diabetes, stroke, and obesity.

Sound rest during caregiving will make or break a day from running smoothly to being so frustrating you won't even be able to think about what needs to be done next. So be prepared to start getting some of the soundest sleep of your life, despite being some of the most challenging times of your life.

Limit Caffeine
Caregiving has a tendency for making us feel anxious, as we have someone else's life in our hands, and we share a lot of their anxiety as well. With this in mind, we want to do everything we can to limit stimulants. If you drink coffee all day while caregiving as I did, your mind is racing when it comes time for bed.

If possible, stop ingesting caffeinated beverages by 3:00 p.m. (soda included.) This will help you sleep easier once your head hits the pillow.

My favorite go to for early afternoon is matcha tea which offers a more consistent, even caffeine buzz so I don't feel jittery later in the afternoon the way too much coffee does.

Have a Cuppa
Borrowing from the Brits here, but a nightly ritual of making a cup of tea, lets your whole body know it's time for bed and to slow down. Make decaf tea before you close the kitchen, then relax. There are some great decaf herbal teas such as: Sleepytime, chamomile or golden milk.

Dim the House Lights Early
I walk past houses at night and see all the lights on Yankee Stadium-style. As a person very sensitive to lighting, it drives me crazy because I know the inhabitants are suffering internally and they don't even know why. That kind of bright light is a sign to the body to turn up the internal volume: Let's get going! –especially in the evening.

Instead, train yourself to dim your house lights starting in the evening hours, long before bedtime. And to really create better sleep and a sense of calm at every turn, that also means put away your phone and computer at least 30 minutes before going to the bedroom. Make the blue lights go away with all the stimulating thoughts that come with social media or the news—anything you indulge in online. Think instead: *Ahhh, tranquility.*

Go to bed
My friend Steve, a holistic healer in NY, always says "if you've had a bad day, go home take a hot bath or shower and go to bed early."

I agree and have used that advice many times. Sometimes the day is just done. Only waking up to a new day will offer a clean slate, time to start anew, make things right, feel good again about the next list of caregiver tasks ahead. Sound rest is an investment in yourself, part of your self-love plan. We are about getting you sound sleep.

Thankfully I have never had problems with sleep; it has always come naturally. I fall asleep and stay asleep once my head hits the pillow. My husband knows I am out when we hit the sheets so he avoids starting deep conversations at bedtime. I am not my best when I don't have a proper eight hours of nighttime sleep, so I want to help you get a good night sleep, especially if it doesn't occur naturally.

Your Bedroom, Your Sanctuary

Once again, we are a broken record repeating: Sleep is essential for a healthy life. With good, restful sleep, caregiving feels effortless. You make better decisions, have fewer mood swings, can roll with the many challenges. You'll let things go more easily and may even find yourself able to laugh more.

So with that in mind, allow your bedroom to become your sanctuary: a place that you look forward to retreating to after a long day. Caregiving is exhausting. You need 7-9 hours of sleep per night to replenish, repair, heal and recover. Try the following tips to transform your bedroom from a last resort into a luxurious one.

Invest in Blackout Shades
Some people lack awareness of their own light sensitivity while sleeping. Even if you think light doesn't affect you, try blackout shades and you will likely sleep even more soundly than before.

Whatever works for you in terms of windows, budget and aesthetics. I can't live without my black out curtains but I hear shades are equally effective.

Keep it Cool
A cool room temperature is best at night. Use a down blanket in cold climates during winter. In warmer climates where it never gets that cold, sleep with a fan. The breeze helps for staying cool. Also consider what kind of pajamas you wear. The fabric and materials matter. During cooler months, opt for flannel or cotton pajamas, as polyester and synthetic blends tend to trap heat. Clothes should follow your advice: breathe. (Soft sleeping shorts and tank tops work for me most of the year.)

Bedding
My husband and I searched for soft cotton sheets for the longest time until we discovered flannel. Flannel sheets provide a comfort I can't describe except *soft and yummy*, even in the heat of the Summer. Now I can't imagine using any other kind of sheets. While this is a personal preference, again, just avoid polyester owing to its heat retention.

Also, make sure your pillows are soft or optimally comfortable. I use two pillows plus one for hugging, so a total of three. Two that vary in softness under my head and the 'hugging' one is firmer and mostly there for those few nights I need extra pillow-love.

Try a Weighted Blanket
"Weighted" blankets aid in the function of rest and recovery. Buy one new or else do what I have done for years, inspired by my yoga practice where blankets are often used on the abdomen. Fold a twin-size cotton throw blanket into a much smaller rect-

angle and rest it on your middle abdominal area at night, over the abdomen and pelvis. There is something soothing and nurturing about using a blanket this way. I used it often in caregiving times as it provided a feeling of being nurtured and hugged which really helped me sleep better.

White Noise
My husband and I have used tranquil sleeping sounds for 20 years. It all started when we lived in Hell's Kitchen, Manhattan, which is very close to Times Square. We discovered white noise machines would drown out the night noise back then, especially on weekends. Now we can't sleep without it. It is just something you get used to over time and then it feels essential. We even use white noise for sleeping when we travel.

Research different types of white noise, then have a listen and see what works for you: natural sounds such as birds, rain, ocean sounds, or else light rhythms. You may purchase a white noise machine or download an app on your phone. Subscriptions to any of the music streaming platforms include white noise songs, artists and playlists. White noise works magic for creating a tranquil environment.

P.S. White noise may also help during the day if you're feeling anxious or want to provide a sense of calm for your mom or dad.

Bedtime!

What I always keep on my Nightstand:

- A new glass of water, nightly
- Almond body oil
- Rose water toner for face-spritzing
- Foot lotion
- Pillow eye mask
- A good book
- Journal + pen
- Scented candle or aromatherapy

Try an Eye Mask & Ear Plugs

An eye mask may be a lifesaver on nights when you feel as though your mind is racing and you just can't seem to quiet it. Maybe you had a stressful day, or your mom or dad had an incident or exchange that keeps playing in your mind... Try an eye mask. I got a very thick and plush one at the airport a few years back. It's the material of a stuffed animal and has some weight to it which I find more comforting and nurturing than the lightweight options in silk or polyester. Your call.

Then there are ear plugs. I wear them to sleep when traveling, especially when Dad moved back to New York, and I was flying back from California every three months those final two years. I used my eye mask with ear plugs for sleeping when I stayed with a friend because of the time zone change and because their household was up very early. I really wanted to make sure I had the best rest possible because I was determined to savor every last minute of memories with my dad, and didn't want sleepless nights getting in the way.

Lotion up & Spritz
After you dim the lights, lotion up. I use almond oil on my body plus I massage a quality foot cream into my feet every night. (Think of how much weight your feet hold and how they carry us all day through our caregiving roles! So, treat them well.)

Next, I spritz my face with rose water, a much less-expensive alternative to toners and the smell is scrumptious. Rose water offers anti-oxidant properties for the skin and the scent also calms the nerves. In fact, you might consider carrying a bottle of rose water with you in your purse or bag when caregiving and spritz yourself often as a self-care treat.

Journal (See Journal section, p 46)
...And the journal makes its second appearance, so take the hint and just write it down.

You might keep a second journal next to your bed only for clearing the mind and use a separate journal that you carry with you for staying organized. Especially when caregiving, there is nothing better than brain-dumping everything from your day onto paper as you are unwinding before bed, yet there is so much to remember for tomorrow. It's also a good practice to get your to-do list onto paper so it's somewhere other than rattling around in your head all night long, as well as purging all that you want to leave behind each day so you don't hold onto it once you start all over again, tomorrow.

Essential Oils
Lavender is a wonderful scent to unwind and relax with. Try a few drops behind your ears, or in your palms vigorously rubbed together and then cupped around your nose and mouth while breathing in slowly.

(Breathe in through your nose for a count of three. Feel your shoulders melt down your back. Breathe out your mouth for a count of three.)

You may also put a couple of drops on your pillow or use diluted portions in spring water in small, portable spray bottles so you don't use too much or soil your linens,.

Some people are sensitive or allergic to lavender, so try it out before purchasing. If you find this applies to you, there are a hundred other essential oils that relax the nervous system. Aromatherapy is essential to caregiving in many circles. I have found it to be another layer of the many things that nurture us and add up to help us (and our parent) stay calm and feel loved.

> **"Legs Up the Wall Pose"**
> It's exactly how it sounds.
> Either lie on the floor or in bed and get close to the wall to put your legs up against it to form an 'L'.
> Do this for 10-15 minutes and your sleep will improve.

Make Your Bed in the Morning

After those delicious seven-to-nine hours of sleep, and your affirmation and mantra, open the blinds to let some light in your room, then make your bed. These two small things will help propel you on a path for a successful day of caregiving. Making your bed is your first task you can feel confident about: Seeing a room with a tidy bed throughout the day is more soothing than a messy one. Plus, there is nothing better than getting into a well-made bed after a long day of caregiving. In that vein, keep a tidy house as best you can, too. Too much subconsciously-perceived chaos in our environment leads us to more anxiety. Disorder also leads to feeling perturbed, too.

Trust yourself
Commit to yourself
Build the confidence you need to
follow through with your self-care.

Pay attention to these little things. They add up!

Take a Nap

Can't sleep?

I love naps. Naps are a shortcut to feeling refreshed. Studies have shown that naps assist in maintaining and even boosting our immune systems by lowering blood pressure, increasing learning ability, and improving memory and performance of complex tasks.

Sometimes I just need to close my eyes for twenty minutes. Afterwards, my mood is elevated and I'm able to continue the day feeling refreshed, empowered—supersonic. I can always tell if I need one, but I grew up with napping so it's part of my DNA. At any age, my dad could look at me and say "Debs, you need a nap. Why don't you take twenty minutes?"

Lo and behold he was always right.

My dad loved to nap too, so we'd occasionally nap at the same time. (Pssst, while caregiving, it's a good practice to nap whenever your parent does if you are able to.)

On the other hand, naps aren't for everybody. My husband can't nap but lying down for twenty minutes refreshes him.

Napping (or lying) on a sofa or a recliner is a much better choice than our bed because we don't want our bodies to get confused. We want to keep the bed and bedroom as our sanctuary for deep sleeping at night. If your only option is to nap in a bed, do that, but don't get under the covers. Use a throw blanket instead, including when napping on a sofa or recliner as well, just to add an essential layer of nurturing. The more you nurture yourself while caregiving, the better.

If you've never tried napping (I know you're out there,) next time you're feeling run down, set an alarm on your phone for twenty minutes. Twenty minutes is the shortest timespan to start with. It takes at least ten minutes to fall asleep, so you're left with at least ten solid minutes of real rest.

When the alarm strikes, rise and shine then ask yourself: *Did it work? How did that feel? Did I fall asleep right away? Did it give me a feeling of calm? Might I do that more often?*

> **Tip:**
> Try sleeping when your parent sleeps, especially naps. This helps squeeze in those required sleep hours to be productive during the day.

In Closing for Self-Care Help

Remember: Self-care is not selfish.

Early on we covered the concept of "filling the well." You've successfully completed the preparation on self-care to make sure your tank isn't empty. You've learned you must nourish and fill your personal well with care, nutritional meals, and proper rest, all while reducing your stress levels. You've learned to give the same attention and care to yourself as you do your loved one so you may become the best caregiver in the world.

Now that we've provided a whole treasure trove of advice how to best protect yourself from becoming sick or depleted while giving your all caring for your parent, you are ready to dive into the next section. Remember, self-care is only half of the circle—180°. We are about to bring the role full circle by diving into the ins and outs of caregiving: its nuances, pitfalls, and demands, including straightforward practical advice for managing the details.

In the end, you'll have completed 360° of Care and should be well on track to becoming the best caregiver you can possibly be.

You've got this.
You are always stronger than you think you are.
I repeat,
YOU ARE STRONGER THAN YOU THINK
you are!

PART TWO
FUELED & READY:
CONNECTED CAREGIVING

It Happens In Stages...

A Caregiver's Perspective: Lexie

I see now we should have looked at things in stages. The stages were:

1. Get Mom a roommate. (That worked for 6 years.)
2. Move Mom into a senior center/ assisted living facility. (She did really well there. Our team was able to remain in place and continue to help.)
3. Mom could no longer take care of herself or understand what medications to take/, when. (She needed extra help a nursing home couldn't provide so this meant moving her into adult foster care.)

We also established the baseline routine for seniors:

- Same time up.
- Same time to bed.
- Same programs on TV.

THE EVER-CHANGING LANDSCAPE

Up to this point, references to my Dad celebrate how jovial he was, but it wasn't always that way. I don't want to paint a picture of perfection, that wouldn't be fair, it's just that I had to think of him that way to get through the many years of caregiving. Accentuating the positive was a means of survival, especially when he was in the nursing home. (Mostly then.) You'll see more balanced stories and pieces of my dad's progression as we continue to examine specifics of the Stages.

A Caregiver's Perspective: Lexie

Many people experience different deteriorating health conditions; there is not going to be 'one box' for each stage. Just because you figured out one stage, the next will come right behind it, requiring you to be just as committed to adjusting again and probably without a formula. As with life, we constantly have to roll with the changes, adapting to the stages of care.

After Dad died, I went through three phases with Mom. My sister and I were unsure whether she would be able to stay in her home, so we thought we'd find her a roommate because mom wasn't a fall-risk or anything. We just wanted her to have evening companionship. We thought *the roommate gets a free room in a house in a lovely neighborhood and they share the kitchen? Totally win-win!*

We put a day schedule together: Mom would visit the local senior center, then lunch with her sister on Tuesdays, and so forth; but we wanted someone who could be there at night so she wasn't alone in the house. (My mom loved her home, the house we grew up in. She was comfortable there and change could have been devastating, especially with mental illness. Besides, we really didn't want to give the home up.)

After three roommates that first year, we re-thought our plan, *Okay, if we can't find Mary Poppins, then this isn't going to work.*

So, we put out all our best intentions for Mary Poppins to manifest, and my God, when Sandy walked through that door, well... The coolest thing was she didn't want to talk to my sister *or* me—she wanted to talk to my mother, Doris!

The other three women we interviewed approached it as if they were going to be caregivers, but that's not what we needed. We only needed companionship for Mom.

It took three "bad" experiences to really get the roommate we wanted. Once we became clear what we were asking for, and by changing the description to really target the kind of person we wanted to attract, Finally! Sandy was the one. We all spent that first afternoon together enjoying each other's company.

A Caregiver's Perspective: Amber

While the social worker was helping me set up the house for my mom's care, she said to me, "Everyone is aware of caregiving as a 'possibility', but it just happens."

At first, that confused me but now that makes sense. I think she meant there is no way to prepare. You just figure out how to get through the mess once you find yourself in it. So don't feel as if anything you're feeling is invalid. For example, my biggest emotion is guilt. I carry a lot of guilt: *Am I doing the right thing? Am I doing enough?* Ahhh, the constant questions you ask yourself trying to figure it all out...

In the beginning stages of her disease, Mom went through a lot of paranoia and started clearing everything out of the house. She didn't know why she was having all this anxiety. Some of our stuff she felt was "possessed." (Dementia produces strange behaviors.) Or she thought she was dying. It was very sad to see.

On the flip side, one thing I would say is it's not all pain—you do learn to laugh. My mom has always been a country music fan and owns a ton of CD's. She will tell me, "I want to listen to George Straight today, or Alan Jackson..." and I'll put it on for her.

One day, while listening to a CD, she just got up and headed for the bedroom, informing me "I'm going to be a back-up singer for Alan Jackson. Are you coming along?" "No," I said, "but I will help you pack."

Is My Home Ready?

There are some home care basics to keep your parent safe if they are living with you or especially if they're living alone.

Dad's "Senior Apartment"

When the apartment building down the street from our condo was being built, we knew it was going to be perfect for my dad. It was a building for seniors and the location was just right. I went there when it was still under construction and spoke to the guys that were working on the site, introducing myself and letting them know my dad was an awesome, cool New Yorker who was already accepted and approved to move there.

"Great!" one lanky Pennsylvanian archetypal construction guy said. "Want me to show you the best apartment in the building? We call it the Penthouse and we all have our lunch up there."

"Oh? Wow, yes, of course." I said blindly trusting his warm smile.

We negotiated one flight of the dusty back stairs of the construction site, then another. I kept thinking: *What have I got into? Should I be wearing a hard hat?* Finally, at the top, we proceeded to the end of the long third floor hallway. As he opened the door, I *knew* I made the right decision. The place was spacious and offered a treetop *and* river view. This was the place: Dad was going to love living here. What more could we want? It brought a tear down my cheek and I burst out "I LOVE IT! Thank You!"

And with *first-day-of-school-level* excitement, I immediately called the manager to make sure Dad got apartment number 305. I felt so proud of what we were able to do for him.

Relish those moments of accomplishment and completion.
Savor the triumphs of caregiving whenever you can.
Even those moments that seem to last forever, won't.
It all goes so quickly.

INTERIM SOLUTION

It would be six months until Dad's "senior apartment" was complete: the early days when Dad wasn't sick yet. He was just worn out and needed love and attention from his daughter to cook him meals and help him get his spirits up. So, he came to live with us until he could move into his new place.

Our office was a separate part of the house with privacy and its own bathroom, so we set up a bed for him in our office. We made a few additional alterations such as putting rails in the shower and one near the toilet. As time progressed, we added a lift for his toilet. These seemed to do the trick until the new place was ready when we repeated some of the enhancements before move-in.

Driving

Should They Still Get Behing The Wheel?

Get ready – your parent is going to fight you on this last straw of independence. (Remember when you were a teenager persuading your parents about using their car? This is role reversal at it's finest.)

At one point my dad was on a couple of medications that definitely made him drowsy. The pill bottle labels plainly said, *do not operate machinery*. I saw that and thought *Oh boy, I don't think he should drive anymore*. Of course, he defended himself when I mentioned it to him.

"I'm fine to drive! After all, it ain't New York, it's Pennsylvania! Lots of greenery and open spaces—not like I'm gonna run anybody over!"

I understood. I tried to stop him, but Dad was *super* convincing. (He was the best storyteller who could talk himself out of any circumstance. That came in handy a lot throughout his life.) At first, his solution was to let his friends drive his shiny red car, figuring it was still a way to get around. Once he got tired of friends driving, he (rather quietly) started driving again—that is, until he got into an accident and totaled his shiny red car. According to the records it wasn't his fault, and thankfully, he wasn't hurt. He didn't even have a scratch and neither did the 90-year-old woman that hit him (also likely a driving risk.) But getting a Saturday morning voicemail after yoga class saying *"Your dad is in the ER"* wasn't exactly my idea of fun.

I wasn't in the car, so I don't know exactly what happened, but the story went: Two elderly individuals come to a four-way stop. "Little old lady" barreled through the stop sign as if it wasn't there, plowing right into Dad's pretty red car.

It could have been much worse, but the totaled car prevented Dad from driving any longer—an absolutely crushing development for him. Yet, with the medications piling up and now other drivers to watch out for, driving was no longer a good idea anyway.

(This stage was prior to him getting cancer. He was still living in his own apartment leading an otherwise "normal" routine. I'd help with some things, but he was primarily independent.)

Nonetheless, we all must know when it's time to help them let go of their car. This is tough, but we are trying to keep them safe the same way they managed to do for us.

A Caregiver's Perspective: Tyler

Mom's biggest frustration happened when she eventually forgot how to put the seat belt on. We'd try to help and she would get so angry: "You guys don't think I can do this!"

We'd reply "No, Mom. We're just trying to help."

Then she would sit silently in that moment—sometimes for a good thirty minutes. At the end of it she would ask, "I'm like this because of the Alzheimer's, right?"

She had the same hard time getting dressed and brushing her teeth—another couple of things she was also in a stage of constant apology about. It was awful:

"I can do this! I can do this!" And then "I'm sorry, I'm sorry."

On some level, she understood what was happening to her and was doing the best she could to try and stay in good spirits.

Mobility

This section's nickname should be *Cane, Walker, Wheelchair*, since that is likely the order you'll follow as you address your parent's increasing mobility limitations.

When Dad first came to live with us, we noticed he was favoring his left and walking a little lopsided. He kind of threw his weight over to one side of his body making his gait very unstable. I assume the pain in his right leg was so miserable that he didn't want to put any weight on it (or admit it,) but it always appeared as if he was about to fall over.

We asked him, "Have you ever used a cane?"

"Don't need one! I'm fine if I use my left leg and don't put weight on the right one."

"Okay," we said. And Charlie ordered him a cane the next day. Canes are a lifesaver to help our favorite adults from falling. The rubber tip on the cane's end hits the ground and sticks to give the person stability. You may choose a single stick or one with four rubber-tipped prongs on the bottom. Our first cane was the single-stick version. It was super stylish, and Dad thought it looked great. Unfortunately, it didn't last. It wasn't enough to keep him stable. We ordered the four-tip model next. This was the one. We chose a color we knew he would like, (winner: his favorite red, to match the red car he owned for many years.) Once he tried that cane, he found it much easier to walk and really embraced using it. He felt safe and so did we.

If you are just arriving at this stage, ask yourself:

Is Mom or Dad willing to use a cane, or do I need to talk them into it?

This is how we talked Dad into the cane:
"If you fall you won't be walking any longer, and you look *really* close to falling. But we know your style. We will get a cane that you *love* the look of." (Or if they prefer to select the style themselves, that's fine too.)

Next tell them, "Everyone uses a cane. It's normal for people as they age."

To cement your justification, find someone your parent is aware of (a celebrity, favorite musician, respected famous person, or even someone they know), and mention "*So-and-so* used a cane for years and never fell once."

What is their style?
As you find their cane, think about what makes them still feel stylish.
And once you get it,
tell them they look debonair or beautiful while using that stylish cane.

Walkers
Eventually, the cane didn't offer enough stability, so we upgraded to a walker.

Walkers are incredible for stability, however, the first thing you learn is the rubber tips on the bottom of the legs wear out fast. The absolute *best* thing to do is get four tennis balls. We were clueless when we first got our walker, until a kind older person told us about the tennis ball trick. Tennis balls come in a package of three, so order *two* packages.

Use a box cutter to cut an X in one side of each tennis ball large enough so it fits over a foot of the walker but small enough the foot doesn't slip out. Be careful of over-cutting.

Each of the four feet of the walker needs its own tennis ball:

- ✦ to help the walker be stable,
- ✦ to quiet noise and avoid scratching floors,
- ✦ and to make for a smoother ride.

Without the tennis balls, your parent will need to 'lift' the walker while using it—a total risk. But once the tennis balls are on the legs, it's smooth sailing, (rather, gliding). They work, so don't skip this step. My dad had his walker for a couple of years which meant we went through quite a few packages of tennis balls.

If your insurance covers walkers, buy a new one and have your insurance pay for it. If not, prepare to spend as they get pricey. Individuals often purchase brand-new walkers after a surgery. Then the person recovers and stops using it, rendering it 'like-new' condition. Most owners don't use their walkers for that long, so there is nothing wrong with buying a used walker, especially one in like-new condition.

You should be able to find a walker for very little cost. They are light enough to pick up yourself. They fold up and fit into a trunk with ease. First check around: *craigslist.com, BuyNothing, Facebook, Nextdoor.com*, and local thrift and consignment shops. (Craigslist is where we found ours cheap.) Also look at: community boards, senior centers, recreation centers, local Masonic Halls, Knights of Columbus, or other philanthropic organizations including Kiwanis, Elks, veteran support groups, the Foreign Legion, or faith-based organizations such as churches, synagogues or mosques, and the rest.

Wheelchairs

Wheelchairs are essential when your parent becomes too weak to support themselves. Hospitals and doctor offices usually have loaner wheelchairs to use when you visit, (especially hospitals,) so before you procure your own, keep track of the places you need to go and call around to make sure all facilities have what you need so there are no surprises.

We obtained our own wheelchair once Dad's chemo treatments made him weak enough that he required one regularly. Dad also didn't have the strength or stability to get himself directly into wheelchairs by himself. The best method we came up with to get him into one involved him getting up on his walker first, then he slowly sat into the wheelchair with my help.

Whenever I took him to appointments, I'd wheel him to the car where he'd maneuver from the wheelchair to the car seat. I would put our wheelchair back in the senior living facility and his walker in our trunk.

Once we arrived at the hospital for chemo appointments, I would get his walker out of the car and then retrieve a loaner wheelchair from the hospital. He needed his walker to get him up from the car and around into their wheelchair (because I couldn't hold him up to get him into the chair by myself.) Believe it or not, this circus routine worked. You may find a different method if your parent is lightweight, or you have other solutions in place to work with.

Where to get a wheelchair?

If you want your own, call around to all the same places referred to above for walkers. We borrowed our wheelchair from the Knights of Columbus by giving them a deposit of $100.00. It was a real lifesaver to have one whenever we needed it. It worked great and was used on many an occasion. They even helped me get it into the car which was so appreciated. (Have you ever lifted a wheelchair? They are heavy, so ask for help.) When we returned it a year and a half later, they refunded our cash deposit.

Tip:
Buy New Canes, as they tend to wear out.
No Reason to Buy New Walkers or Wheelchairs, (especially if you find 'like-new' condition.)

A Caregiver's Perspective: Erin

One thing I will say is now I know I can do anything! Caregiving at this deep a level is super empowering.

House Readiness

Bathroom

The bathroom is the most functional, least-pretty environment serving caregiving. (Say goodbye to your dream spa, at least temporarily, while retrofitting your space to accommodate the new needs of your extended family's use.)

Checklist: What do I need?

- Do you need to install a rail in the tub/ shower?
- Do they need a rail near the toilet?
- Shower bench?
- Extended shower hose?
- Do they need a toilet lift or boost? A commode?

Revisit the walker and wheelchair resources. This first-step may save you a lot of money and is worth the time to research. We found a brand-new commode on Craigslist.com. Sometimes individuals buy these items in preparation for events to come but don't end up using them. It's worth a try; you may get lucky.

At-Home Bathing
When Dad was getting sick but still able to stay in his apartment down the street from Charlie and me, Charlie gave him showers.

We set up the shower bench, rails, and installed an extended shower hose, but my favorite purchase was a fluffy, royal blue velour robe (after all, Dad was royalty.) When Charlie finished helping Dad shower, they would open the bathroom door and out rolled royalty *full-steam ahead*, tennis-ball-footed walker in-hand. I'd break into song ("Rocky's Theme") while steam poured out of the bathroom and off my strong father's head, the only exposed body part since his floor-length royal blue robe covered him from head to toe.

Every time, Dad's ear-to-ear smile made us feel as if we just received a gift straight from the Universe. (We had, all three of us.)

If your parent prefers a bath, your mom or dad's mobility stage, along with their stability, strength, and balance will determine if taking a bath is safe. Baths may be problematic unless you have a solution to lift them. You can buy an automatic pulley system that has a sling and aides in placing them in the tub, although, even with lifts, you may still require assistance. Getting in and out of a slippery bath full of water involves great slipfall risk. Tub-side rails aren't accessible once your parent is seated unless they have enough strength to grab on and pull themselves up and out.

You might also consider a bench in the tub along with a rail attached to the side of the bath so they can grab on and lift themselves up while you guide them from behind. Additionally there are "handicap" shower stalls that work well.

There are advantages to be had by building a new bathroom to accommodate them which offers a wider range of options. Consider installing a bench in the shower stall, or a curbless entry to wheel a wheelchair into the stall while using the shower hose. (They used this method in the nursing home.) The beauty of *no tub* options mean no maneuvering or heavy lifting required, which keeps them safer (the name of the game.)

Next step is understanding whether they can bathe themselves once they're in. Again, it depends how far along are they in terms of mobility, stability and balance. Generally speaking, assistance will be in order lathering up their body and shampooing their hair. When Charlie helped Lenny shower, he would use a shower brush with a handle and scrub Dad's back, then hand him a soapy washcloth so Dad could wash his own privates. When shampooing, use baby shampoo because odds of getting soap in their eyes are good. This is also where that handheld showerhead / hose combo comes in handy to help them rinse.

A Caregiver's Perspective: Amber

Scents + Shampoo
Mom always had a sensitivity to smells so we used unscented products, soaps, detergents, and such. Recently I found some smells actually trigger moods and my mom's state of mind, such as when I ask her a question after a scent hits the air, she answers quick and snippy: *"I know!"* in a backtalking tone where I know she's upset. So, I started washing her hair with baby shampoo. Her hair was naturally thick, but age and the medications she takes have made her hair thin, so even with the baby shampoo, I still find the smell

triggers her so, I searched for unscented baby shampoo and eventually found some that works.

Bathing + Dressing
Removing the full-length mirror has really helped my mom. At this point she is rail thin and every time she looked in the mirror she would say "Why do I look like this?"

I would say "Momma, we're all going to look that way eventually."

Next, what I have found to work is bathing her in stages.

+ I give her a washcloth to wash her private parts when she goes potty.
+ She's okay when I'm with her in the bathroom for brushing her teeth.
+ Then I will wash her back and such in the bedroom.
+ I won't give her a hand mirror until after I brush her hair and she looks pretty.

For dressing, it took me about 2-3 months of trial and error to discover I should only give mom two choices for clothing, and the options need to be only plain shirts without patterns because the patterns confuse her. For example, I let her choose her favorite shirt with a lizard on it and she kept asking me all day if the lizard was real. Fifteen minutes to get dressed became an hour and a half.

Now I say, "Which shirt?" and lay two on the bed: "White or Pink?" Then the bottoms: "Grey pants or black skirt?"

My Mom is such a prideful person, things such as grooming are a big deal to her. Mom always liked Mary Jane shoes, but they don't work anymore. She really needs slip-ons. I found her a really cute pair and now she is able to put them on herself. This is huge for her. It really helps her keep her dignity.
"Yeah, I did it!" my mom says each time.

These limited choices really helped, plus preventing her from seeing herself in the full-length mirror.

A Caregiver's Perspective: Lexie

Grooming for Mom
Mom loved baths, but as she got more and more disabled, baths weren't possible any longer. It was hard for my mom to move around a lot because of her arthritis and obesity. She really fought me on the showers. I had to sternly say to her "You have to take a shower. No one likes a stinky old woman!"

So, we put a bench in the shower and also got a showerhead with a long hose that had a *massage* mode. I would make sure we showered mom every two days.
On the shower days and also the in-between shower days I would prepare a soapy washcloth for her then she would wash her own privates and underarms.

We tried to make showering a pleasurable experience. She loved the little pulsation on her neck.

Her **toenails** also needed to be done after the shower as that's when they are soft and easier to cut. I would have her sit on the toilet in the bathroom and every other week, I would cut her nails—especially because if we didn't, she got ingrown toenails and couldn't walk.

Fingernails. She always liked to grow her nails long and paint them. She used to keep her hands well-manicured and groomed. But since she wasn't well or as mobile, I kept them short for many reasons. When long, she couldn't keep them clean which may have led to infection. Plus, she really hated having her nails "done" by us, so we would cut them when we did her toenails, after the shower as well.

Hair + Lipstick. My mom was glamorous in her prime—she resembled Liz Taylor. She always kept herself up, looking stylish and fabulous until she gained a lot of weight from the medications. That really slowed her down and made things harder to keep up. Once I was her caregiver, we kept her hair short and sharply groomed. And my mom still always wore lipstick.

My advice: if your parent is resistant to bathing, find an experience that is pleasurable to both of you because no one likes to wash a cat. I found joy with the water massage setting and she really enjoyed it, too.

Shaving Dad's Head

Dad had a full head of hair almost all of his life. I always picture Dad with the best set of dark curly locks springing from his head. Now that he was older and unwell it was thinning a little, but still had bounce. Regardless, he always looked handsome.

When Dad was first diagnosed with lymphoma, the cancer hospital had my dad and me watch a video on what to expect and how to prepare yourself for cancer treatments. I will never forget us sitting alone in that cold, small room with a TV and watching that terrible 'teaching' video. We both felt sick as it "guided" us through all the awful things to come. (As if we didn't know?)

We were so upset by it, we agreed afterwards we needed to shave Dad's head while he still had hair, (the only useful takeaway from that video.) At least this approach avoids the worse alternative: clumps of hair falling out as constant reminders of how their body is reacting to their sickness.

Once we recovered from watching the video, I was a little afraid how to broach the topic again, so one day I simply packed Charlie's shears in my bag and took them to Dad's house.

"Do you want to shave your head?"

"Yes."

No other words were exchanged.

(Dad and I had this relationship where even though we loved to talk, if we agreed on something that was sad or difficult, we'd just proceed in silence. I think growing up with a mom with mental illness made these awkward moments seem matter of fact, as in, *just do it because it makes sense and that's it. No use going on about it.*)

Minutes later, he sat on his kitchen chair, towel around his shoulders, feet grounded on the floor in stoic duty.

And so it began. I turned that electric razor on. Never having done this before, I went slowly, steadily following the shape of his head, guiding the blades from back-to-front and back again. Each lock fell to the floor, huddling together in a single ball as if to let me know it was okay... we were okay...

I tried to avoid Dad noticing the tears rolling down my face. I couldn't help thinking *I'm the parent, now*. It was my turn to protect Lenny: to make sure *he* was okay, that he was safe...

> *Add another Post-it to your fridge saying:*
> *You've got THIS!*
> *Remember, daily visual reminders*
> *are incredible for helping us:*
> *1- stay focused on the tasks at hand, and*
> *2 - give good care to yourself and your parent.*

Daily Routines

Cooking, Cleaning, Food Shopping & Laundry

As the self-starter type, I try to do it all—not a healthy approach to caregiving.

Dad was at his own apartment down my street when his health started declining. Once he was diagnosed with cancer and started chemo, he was no longer capable of "all of the things," so I inevitably found myself food shopping, cooking, cleaning, and doing laundry—literally breaking my back to keep up. His apartment was the last on the top floor, all the way down the hall, furthest from the elevator.

One day I admitted *I need help*. First, I looked for someone to clean his apartment while I ran Dad to all of his doctor and chemo appointments, (plus managed my photography business and my own home life.) I found a Craigslist post from a woman who advertised that she cleaned using only natural products.

Oh, yes, right up my alley. This must be the person. Sure enough, Rachel was.

Who is Rachel, you ask?

Rachel was a compassionate and mighty strong woman (emotionally and physically) who already raised five now-grown children. Rachel grew up a practicing Amish with extended family on a functioning animal and crop farm in Lancaster, Pennsylvania.

When we met Rachel, she was ex-Amish, no longer practicing nor living on a farm. She had just started pursuing a career in real estate and possessed a strong sense of community alongside a deep care for helping others. We were beyond lucky to find her as she truly cared for my Dad.

In fact, both *really* loved to talk, chatting it up and spending time together. As far as growing up, she and Dad came from opposite ends of the spectrum, (country/ city,) so they were enthralled by each other's differences. My dad loved hearing about her farm life and she, in turn, enjoyed hearing all his New York City stories. My dad even started reading as many library books on the Amish as he could get his hands on because he wanted to learn all he could about Rachel's experiences.

Even though I initially paid Rachel to clean, she would bring homemade food to Dad's apartment. We started finding incredibly delicious home-cooked Amish surprises in the fridge such as a chicken and corn soup that I have yet to taste an equal.

One day, Rachel saw me carrying Dad's laundry bag into the elevator and chased me all the way to my car yelling, "Do you want me to help you with the laundry?"

"What? Really? YES!" I exclaimed, thinking the gods were cheering us both on.

When your parent's health really starts deteriorating, you become aware of the many things that were taken for granted that suddenly need to get done. Chores that come with living life seemed simple when your parent was able to do them, but they soon escalate into much heavier burdens to manage. So, what started as cleaning assistance also became meals, laundry, and eventually even minor trips to the store. Truly Heaven-sent, I was ever so grateful for every fleeting bit of help. I paid Rachel in cash for the cleaning and then for extra services she began to take on, and eventually if she was going to pick up anything from the store, I gave her a wad of cash in advance.

"But you are giving me so much extra cash?" she would say, followed anxiously by, "Don't worry, I'll keep the receipts for everything."

And I would reply, "Just bring back whatever you don't use. No big deal."

She couldn't understand how I had so much trust in her. And I couldn't understand why she didn't understand. For whatever reason, I trusted her whole-hardheartedly, and eventually she accepted this. Rachel did so much more out of a love for Dad that was so kind and deeply appreciated by us. She helped us tremendously and we are all forever grateful for Rachel.

We all need a Rachel. And while I sincerely hope you find someone similar to assist you in all your domestic duties, finding the right person to clean the house or help with laundry and shopping takes some work. We were incredibly lucky, but you must be cautious about who you let into your parents' home. When looking, ask neighbors, look at community boards, and check with the local senior center.

Once you find someone, especially if sourced from a bulletin board or anonymous resource such as the Internet, ask around to see if anyone else has used this person. Checking references is very important. Even though we don't like to think about it, there is a lot of elder abuse we need to be aware of, as well as the straightforward crimes such as theft.

Meals

In the beginning of the journey, it was difficult to understand the exact role I needed to play. We are tempted to just "take things over" and run them. What I needed to do was to give Dad control of his own life.

Meal prep and proper eating is a slippery slope, and it seems every caregiver goes through their own trials and tribulations. My goal became getting Dad through his chemo treatments successfully without him getting too sick in the process. I tried to guide him with my own health and wellness knowledge: asking him if he was willing to eat organic, go gluten-free and maybe even green juice every day... but I didn't plan to force them on him. I would just make some of these items 'available' in the hopes he might warm up to them.

One day I arrived at his apartment and to start buttering him up, straight-out asked whether he was willing to make those adjustments and he answered YES! (He said *YES!*)

Following that conversation, it was a miracle. I'd show up to his apartment and he'd be juicing. What a sight: my Italian father making juice in his little apartment kitchen!

The first thing he would say when I walked in was "Guess what I was just doing?"

I'd put that ol' role reversal into action ignoring the juicer on the counter and say "What? Making donuts?"

He would answer "Juicing!" beaming with a big smile on his face then proceed to tell me what he put in it. (Exactly like Charlie and I did when we first started.)

> ## A Caregiver's Perspective: Erin
>
> If someone dropped off a lasagna, it was a gift from God: OK, minus one thing to worry about *today*!

> ## A Caregiver's Perspective: Amber
>
> When Mom wants to make tea, I ask "Do you want to do it?" That's the hard thing, in this middle stage she still wants to do things, still wants to feel useful. I don't just want to tell her No all the time.
>
> So I follow-up with, "Okay let's do it."
>
> Then I monitor her. I let her sweeten it or tell me what

cup she wants, but once she gets to the cabinet to pick her cup, she often looks at me blankly and says, "Why am I here again?"

The other day she sweetened her tea with raw grits instead of sugar. I laugh just so I can keep things light.

Another time I was collecting trash around the house to take out, and my mom misbehaved the whole time—like a bad kid. Afterwards, I needed to pick up some personal items at Walgreens and finally scolded her, "Mom, do NOT move out of this space while I'm gone. I don't want you to fall. I don't want you to go to the hospital."

"Right," she said—and just gave me this 'look.'

I prodded, "OK, if you *do* have to move, what are we going to do?"

"Use my walking cane."

I said, "That's right."

So I start walking down the block and already see her in the window, and now I'm praying: *Dear God, don't let her be on the floor when I come back.*

I get home and instead, she's in bed with the covers pulled up to her neck.

"What happened? I *know* something happened!"

She said, "I fixed a snack."

So, I go into the kitchen. Things are all over the place, a total mess. She had opened a can of corn, added a half-eaten banana and topped it with a glob of mayo.

Stepping into that situation a year ago, I would have yelled "Why did you do that?" But now I can be okay with it. Now I simply ask, "Did you use your cane?"

That time she lit up: "Yes! I did! I remembered! And I didn't fall!"

So I went back to the kitchen, took some deep breaths, and proceeded to clean up.

I am also always trying to give my mom little things to do so she isn't just sitting on the sofa all day, either. For example, a package arrived in the mail that contained bubble wrap, and she asked me, "May I pop them?"

"Of course."

She popped them until they were all gone, then was tired and took a nap.

A Caregiver's Perspective: Val

Before I moved in, I started to cook all of Mom's meals. I would make a few days' worth of food and bring it all over so she could just easily heat it up for her meals.

After moving in with her, I had to trick Mom into eating every day.

Once she became weaker and unable to come to the dinner table, my daughter and I brought our trays into her bedroom to eat with her. Whenever she attempted to not finish a perfectly good meal, we would estimate how many forkfuls were left on her plate (we called them "fork-*fulls*.") We always made the count low-enough that she could be confident she could complete the amount. And it worked!

Eating together as a family and bringing activities to Mom's bedside encouraged her to eat. She knew that she was a very important and honored member of our family. This resulted in her healthy weight gain and retention. Her kidney function even increased.

Snacks during the day also helped her to regain a healthy weight. She really liked my "gourmet" sandwiches. They were full of vegetables with a few slices of meat and a thick slice of extra-sharp cheddar cheese. Her favorite was when I baked meatloaf and browned it in a skillet served on toasted bread for her sandwich.

It was my pleasure indeed.

*Be good to yourself.
Don't forget to breathe.
Repeat your daily mantra.
You are perfect.*

The Support Squad

A Caregiver's Perspective: Susan

It's hard to ask for help, especially those of us who are independent, self-starter "*I-can-do-it-all*" types. Let people help you, Remember, there are people who want to help!

Sometimes you're so overwhelmed with caregiving you can't delegate. You get caught up emotionally and become impractical. You can't see the forest through the trees.

How To Build Your Team

Step One: Surrender
It's incredible how we think we can do it all when we start this journey of caregiving. That is, until one day you find yourself so exhausted you can hardly get out of bed. This happened to me and was my breaking point. I finally knew I needed to ask for help.

Don't allow this to happen to you. Please get help as soon as possible.

Step Two: Ask
One of the best ways to care for yourself and your parent is to ask for help and form your PERSONAL team, first. By doing so, you create balance for both you and your parent. Everyone needs downtime: to be, to breathe, and to continue engaging with our lives, friends, and hobbies. Our parent also needs other persons in their life to engage with

and create a balance of their own. We think we're enough for them, but it's much healthier for cognitive and overall health to interact with many individuals. This makes you both happier.

If I did it all over again, I would get my support in place first. Having more people to count on prevents always searching for more to help. That said, the ever-changing landscape of caregiving means individuals will fall off your list, too. Individuals always have new commitments develop in life (or just don't want to help anymore,) which may be upsetting to you, but is to be expected.

Understand others' priorities are not a negative reflection of you or your parent. Conditions differ for everyone. Depending on their comfort level with how sick your parent is: their possible triggers and sensitivities, or other obligations they must absorb, (including costs such as transportation, activity fees, refreshments, contributions, even emotional costs,) ongoing meetups can become a crap shoot. Establish what YOU can afford out of the gate, as that may help keep participants in your circle as well.

Also, only certain friends are the right kind of friend to support you during this time. I remember when my mom passed, instead of saying, "I'm here for you," one of my friends said, "Let me know when you're over it and we will get together then." That hurt. Maybe she just didn't know what to say? Some may not be in the right position to support you. Some don't know how to. That's okay.

At times I felt extremely alone caregiving for Dad. I recall one occasion where I sat down to write a group e-mail that said *Please help me* to every friend I had. But I stopped myself because I had a really hard time asking for help.

I did have my wonderful husband, but he was going through his own adjustments as he had loved my dad for almost 20 years, too. Even though there are people around you, your bond with your parent makes it just the two of you in a way. You're so enmeshed and so involved in their life, you even share the same emotions. But your parent's emotional support isn't available to you anymore, including simple moral support. And we need this. I had one amazing long-distance friend who was there for me throughout, thick and thin, until the very end. A simple weekly phone call did wonders.

So again, it's best to be prepared for lots of changes along the way. Go slow and be kind to yourself.

Step Three: What do you need help with?
Don't do everything. I should have thought this way from the start. It would have saved a lot of exhaustion. Asking for help is wise, brave and above all, necessary. I keep saying this, but burnout is real and recovery time is real, too. So be realistic. Asking for help does not mean you're weak or incapable.

At first Dad would go food shopping with a friend and was able to cook some meals. Later, I took on food shopping, then cooking, then laundry and cleaning house, all the while, taking him to unending appointments.

First, list which practical things you need help with, depending on which stage your parent is in and whether they're shopping for food, cooking their own meals, doing laundry, cleaning house or even driving. Start with this handy checklist and tailor based on who else you need:

- Food shopping
- Cooking meals
- Laundry
- Cleaning the house
- Exercise, including walking
- Socializing with a friend, neighbor, family member
- Going to doctor appointments
- Scheduled home visits
- Daily phone calls for support
- Outings: park, restaurants, movies, theater, concerts, Senior Center visits, faith services

Establish a Support Budget

Next, look at your budget. Do you have one? If so, how much do you have to spend each month? Look at your parent's finances and see how much can be allotted for help.

Once you know the monthly amount of money you can spend, determine where the resources should go. See how much help is available from volunteers and then who you can afford to hire. Keep in mind family members and friends may volunteer to help with your *to do* list as well. (Remember: Muster up the courage to ask.)

Don't have a budget to work with? That's okay. Empathizers will volunteer, so don't give up. You may need to get creative, but some more ideas are on the way... keep reading.

Note: My dad didn't have much, but the $200 a month he could spare went a long way.

Form The Team

Who loves you, baby? -Telly Savalas

Great place to start: make a list of who loves your Mom or Dad. Who has been involved in their life over the years?

Siblings, aunts, uncles, cousins, family friends, your parent's friends, neighbors, your own friends that know and love your parents, familiar contacts around the community, faith-based locations they have attended or still do, groups they belonged to, social communities they belonged to. (Example: Dad was very involved in the Knights of Columbus, so it felt right reaching out to them when he moved back to New York.)

When you're done, ask your parent if they can think of anyone else to add.

Become a detective. We often realize we don't know all the aspects of our parent's life until we start digging.

When Dad retired, he volunteered to feed the homeless and befriended a woman named Mary he spoke highly of over the years. Turned out Mary was the director of a church organization that ran the program to feed the homeless—a real dynamo. She and my dad became great friends over many years. When Dad got sick and was back in New York, they reconnected and spoke on the phone. Both were up in age, and Mary wasn't that well either, but she visited on the days she felt okay.

Add to the list: **Who can commit to a weekly phone call?** It requires picking up the phone or logging onto video for fifteen minutes or more, just chatting. You fill in the schedule gaps with friendly check-ins.

My dad had this address/phone book—the sweetest, messiest thing you've ever seen. Coffee stains, torn pages, phone numbers written on tops of pages, not neatly in the rows or boxes so you could understand it or find anyone. I'd visit Dad and ask who he'd talked to lately, especially if I could tell he was feeling lonely and sad.

Sometimes he said no one. Other times he might say "Well, Stella called..." (his sister- in-law from Florida.) Then, I knew it was coming: "Debs, get me my address book."

He would always come up with someone from the past. I would always thumb through his personal mess looking for their number with no luck, which always ended with him saying "Give me that."

Within minutes, I'd be dialing someone's number on his flip phone for a friendly phone chat.

I have to say, phone calls were more uplifting than one thinks. It feels good when playing detective and makes someone's day. My friend's grandma always said, "a phone call is just like a visit." So, when you can't make it to see Mom or Dad, give them a call and encourage others to do the same.

Once Dad was very ill and bedbound, I would remind each member of our small team to call him on a regular basis. My father appreciated every call he received and would gleefully recite the details of each. Your parent may do the same. It's the little things in life that add up to the whole of their experience.

How to ask friends, family, and neighbors to pitch in:
Always begin by inquiring what kind of time they have to contribute:

- Can they commit to one afternoon a week to have lunch with mom or dad?
- Do they have an hour a week to take them to the community center or senior center for bingo or any other routine events? Maybe they have an indoor pool at the facility?
- Who has time to pick up groceries? This may be curbside pick-up where you order, and they just pick them up. (Unless regular delivery service is in your budget instead.)
- Who can make a meal once a week and drop it off? Something easily heated.
- If your parent attends any religious services, who can assist them in getting there and back, or even join them?
- Ask who can be put on the list for the important task of taking Mom or Dad to a routine doctor appointment.
- Can someone pick up medications at the pharmacy? (Or you might consider having them delivered.)
- Can someone volunteer to help clean? Or do you need to hire someone?
- Can someone commit to doing laundry once a week? Even if it's "just towels" or one recurring load. Or does laundry need to be dropped off at a laundromat? (A great option if you have the budget. Even better if the service offers pick-up and delivery.)

If your parent is in a care facility or a nursing home, you still need to build a team. The facility usually takes care of the cooking, cleaning and laundry, nonetheless, these are all items you need to check on regularly to verify they are getting done.
(*See Chapter V - Nursing & Care Facilities.*)

Friends

Set time aside for you to spend alone with friends. Schedule a date at least once a week to meet up with a friend, a group of friends, a family member, even a neighbor. Who in your circle are good listeners? Who will be supportive and have compassion for what you're experiencing? The right friends will make you relax or offer a helping hand. Maybe you can find some time to laugh and have fun in the process, too.

(I can hear you right now: *How am I going to find the time for that?*)

We've said it before in Self-Care but it is worth repeating in Caregiving, too: Learning to delegate responsibilities is an important skill to develop. Find someone who can sit with your parent during that window, or at least check in on them, (depending on the situation and how much caregiving is required of you.) Two hours will make a world of difference for both of you. Your parent wants you to enjoy your life, even while caregiving for them. I know my dad wanted this for me as much as I wanted it for him and myself.

A Caregiver's Perspective: Lexie

It is essential to put a team of caregiver persons together. You may think: "Oh, my mom's sister or my cousin would never want to be involved with caring for her..." Yet, ask them, they may surprise you.

When we went to ask Auntie Babe, we said "Mom needs someone on Saturday afternoon. She has a big void in her day. Would you mind taking her for a cup

> of coffee and a pastry"?
>
> "I would love to!" she replied. So every Saturday at 4:30 p.m., Auntie Babe would come and take mom to get coffee and a pastry.
>
> Plus, our Auntie Dodie would come to the house every Sunday for an hour, too. She did that until the end.

What is referred to as "community opportunities" involves casting a wide net into the public and watching the creative ways different individuals get involved. It requires keen organization to get everyone on a calendar in their specific "spot," however, remember that there are quite a few persons that love your parent. People orbiting in your parents' life may surprise you, especially how many will say "Yes" to things you didn't consider requesting. You must be willing to ask. Unless you ask, you won't know who is willing to contribute what. Then pretty soon, you will have put together this little quilt of helpers. You may still have to hire additional persons to fill in gaps but what a tapestry! Once a month I would write Dad's whole calendar to manage the schedule and it always moved me.

> ### A Caregiver's Perspective: Susan
>
> This was all new territory for me and I needed support. Even questions such as *Is this medication good?* Or, *my brother is being difficult, how do I manage?*

I would call my cousin Nan for medical advice from time to time: very helpful as she was in the field. And of course, I could ask my therapist about anything personal I was dealing with, but I couldn't call her in the middle of the night when most things were racing through my head.

So, in my particular instance, calling the **Alzheimers.org help line** was most helpful. Another Godsend. It's available 24 hours and I found them to be knowledgeable, helpful, and compassionate— especially when I was down in Georgia and having difficulty with my brother and sometimes the other caregivers.

I'd estimate that I called the Alzheimer's Hotline *hundreds* of times—many of those times at 1:00 a.m. or 2:00 a.m. Of that entire time, only 2 or 3 times did I get someone I didn't click with.

A Caregiver's Perspective: Erin

Usually, Mom and I couldn't do anything together as someone always had to be with Dad. Thankfully, we received support from the Jacobsons, some really good family friends who lived close by.

The Jacobsons would call and say "Hey, I have a four-hour block today without anything going on. Why don't I come and hang out with Dennis? I can read to him while you two girls go to lunch, or get a pedicure, or go do something."

Because they were so specific in their help offering, it was much easier to say yes. That was such a blessing.

Now if someone asks *me* how to help in a similar situation, I say "Be specific with what you can do. Offer to bring them meals, or take their laundry, or help with cleaning the house..."

A Caregiver's Perspective: Tyler

Look for local support groups. My sisters and I found a support group at a church. Once we all went together, we realized it's so helpful to hear what other individuals are going through. When you hear the public's stories, you know you're not alone.

Local Community

As you're asking around your team for visitors, drop-bys, meetups and such, let others know *so and so visits on Saturday*, and suggest *Would you visit on Sunday?* It's human nature when individuals see other individuals involved, they somehow want to be part of it.

In New York, there was a woman who was around my age that would visit once a week with my dad when he was in the nursing home. I didn't know her or how they met and was never aware she would visit him until one time she showed up and I was in his room.

"Oh, you must be Debs," she said warmly. "I love your dad! He tells the best stories."

Apparently, she had been visiting him weekly for months. I was so touched. So just realize as you build your team, more may offer to help – forming a chain- reaction.

Depending how active your parent is at any given stage will determine how many activities they can attend. If they are inactive or unable to attend events or group activities, reach out to the leaders of the groups to see if they might suggest someone that could share the group's updates, or possibly even visit your parent at home or the care facility to talk about that particular interest. There are a lot of supporters that want to help out there in the world, you just have to find them.

- ✦ Check for community boards at local places of worship, (churches, synagogues, mosques, etc.), retail stores, and other high-traffic places in the local area.
- ✦ Is there a recreation center in your community? What resources do they have?
- ✦ What does your/ their local library offer?
- ✦ Is there a senior center in your area? What kinds of groups do they have for seniors?

A Caregiver's Perspective: Penelope

If you go back to basic human evolution, it was teams that allowed for human survival. People supporting each other... So, once I got to the point where I was really tired and needed a break—to go out for walks... to just go into town and have a coffee... you know, all of those basic kinds of mental breaks one needs—we paid a family member, the granddaughter of my cousin, to come look after Mom two mornings a week.

This break allowed my daughter, Suji, and me to take time off. Sometimes I would take Suji to her dad's office, as she needed time away from that constant caregiving scene, too. So that all worked out beautifully.

A Caregiver's Perspective: Erin

Go to a Therapist. I assure you this will help, especially when you're being responsible with someone else's life as a caregiver. It helped me tremendously.

More Resources To Ask For Help:

- Alzheimer's association- alz.org
- Cancer association- cancer.org
- Parkinson's association- parkinson.org
- Meals on Wheels -mealsonwheelsamerica.org
- Care.com
- The local library & senior center
- The local recreation & community centers
- For buying furniture, walkers, and so forth: Craigslist.org
- Silver Sneaker care for seniors- This is something that is connected to certain health insurance plans for the 65+ community and may be part of your plan. Check out your insurance companies as they may have additional benefits or programs for seniors.
- Faith-based organizations

Boundaries

As with any relationship, boundaries are consequential. It's important to maintain a sense of Self during this time. When caring for a parent, parent-child lines tend to get blurry both ways, so boundaries become critical to draw for our own sanity as well as that of our parent. Boundaries also need to be put in place for all the persons sharing our parent's and our lives. The minute you start to feel suffocation from all the duties you need to perform for your mom or dad is the precise moment you should step back, pause, re-evaluate and change your approach.

When people are sick, they feel vulnerable. There is loneliness as well as isolation with being sick. Sudden changes may lead to quick depression. As caregivers, we are already hyper-sensitive and attuned to what's going on with our parent—often at our own expense. This is where the self-care practice becomes so important. Understanding your limits, your parent's limits and your team's will help things flow. Open communication with those in your squad will make or break these trying times. Remind all teammates to please keep this in mind.

The idea here is avoid judging yourself or anyone else and avoid taking things personally when individuals fall off (as they will. It happened to us several times, and each time my dad and I took it personally and eventually learned how to protect ourselves better.)

Our little team was small but mighty. Everyone played a part, "had a role in the play" if you will. Even the smaller roles were equally as important and made up the threads of the quilt. Roles such as: call once a week; send a card in the mail; visit with a sandwich; an afternoon to watch tennis; drop off a book from the library...

Individuals have other commitments in their lives and may not see the importance of either their relationship with your parent or visiting your parent. I advise letting participants know upfront that their commitment is very important to you and your parent, and while you know things will come up in their lives, to please communicate directly at their earliest convenience when things change.

The following is an example of a situation that started great then went off the rails:

A very good friend of the family that my dad treated as a son because he had known this gentleman since the guy's birth—even helped raised him to some degree—re-surfaced when Dad moved back to New York. The guy showed up every week with a sandwich to visit with Dad in the nursing home. Sometimes he would even bring one of his kids. Dad *loved* these visits and came to rely on them because they brought him so much joy. The guy was part of our circle, our squad, our tribe.

Until one day, this guy we've known our whole lives just *disappeared.*

Dad and I called him for days. He didn't answer his phone. Weeks went by. My father was so concerned something happened to him.

We eventually found out the guy was okay—no accident, injury, illness or emergency— nothing of the sort. We were relieved to find out he was 'fine' after knowing nothing for weeks. What wasn't fine was that he just stopped calling, answering his phone, and never came to visit again. This person visited my father once a week for over a year, then out the blue just halted with zero explanation. Dad never got over it. He talked about it all the time, "What did I do? What did I say? May I tell him I'm sorry?"

Dad never got the chance, which seemed cruel to me. By that point, Dad was bedbound, so he lived for the little moments, the hours here or there that would help him make it through the rest of the day, night, week... I was furious with this person and yet, I had to let it go. We both did.

The moral of the story is, you need to build a tribe and the right tribe, which makes all the difference. Sometimes, we need certain individuals on our team more than others. But everyone needs to communicate openly and respect each other's boundaries. It took a few tries, but we got it, and you will get it too. It's all part of the ever-morphing caregiving journey.

A Caregiver's Perspective: Susan

Siblings may certainly be supportive at times, but they come with their own set of challenges. It all comes down to management. Who is good at what? Who can take this on?

The more specific you are in asking people how they can help, the more successful you will be. I equate everything with fundraising since that is the world I know: You don't go to a bread company and ask them to sponsor a meat event. In other words, match your ask with the right person.

For example, having my brother deal with doctors was a nightmare because he doesn't know the right questions to ask. Consequently, if our mother needed to order something from the store (Walmart was the only store there), then that was a perfect task for him because he could just pick it up.

When it comes to being a caregiver, try and be still. It helps you trust yourself. Then go with your gut. I also like to say "You can't get oranges at the hardware store," meaning once I stopped expecting my brother to be who I wanted him to be through all of this and then accepted him for who he was instead, our relationship changed.

A Caregiver's Perspective: Lexie

Some persons are just not up for caring for their parent. There are multiple reasons: it may be selfish; or it may just be *I can't deal with it and I have the money to put Mom or Dad in a nursing home/ senior care facility, so that's what I'm going to do.*

I am a community organizer, a nurturer, a karma yogi, and I care for people. I was born with a lot of caregiver qualities. My sister, on the other hand, is not a caregiver, so this role was very hard for her—especially that we ended up caring for my mother for 14 years. She still resents that experience until this day.

I don't recommend what my sister did. If you or a person in your care-sphere are getting resentful, or just aren't suited for the caregiving role, find a team that is.

A Caregiver's Perspective: Tyler

When the neurologist gave us Mom's diagnosis he said "this disease is going to make or break your family." We constantly kept this in mind because there were many moments when we didn't want to talk to each other anymore, where some of us felt as though one was always doing more.

My sisters and I would remind each other: *Remember when the neurologist said this will make or break our family?* He was absolutely right, especially if you don't have a very strong foundation.

We were tested so many times with this disease, trying to take care of mom while trying to live our own lives. It was definitely a journey for us, because we are all in different seasons of our lives. One sister is ten years older and my other sister is two years older, so I'm the youngest.

I really was just starting to live and then this hit us and took a whole other turn. It was so different from what life was supposed to be for us all.

A Caregiver's Perspective: Amber

When my dad was sick, my mom and I had each other. But later, it was very tricky trying to figure out my support systems as sole caregiver for Mom. Even though some mean well, you can't let everybody in. It's about creating this safe space for the person you're caring for on all levels.

Sometimes individuals that mean well might really stomp on your emotions. They'll say, "I'm going to drop by" forcing me to say, "No, please don't drop by

> at that time," because it resets the whole clock of our care routine.
>
> I know they mean well, but I also know it's going to debunk the system in place. As a people-pleaser, it's hard to say no. My focus was on how well Mom is functioning because that determined how well I'm functioning.
>
> It was one of those life lessons I had to adapt to really quickly, and it hurt. There's real loneliness in being a caregiver.

Lenny & Me: The Letdown

Right before Dad moved from his home to the first care facility, he was falling all the time. His neighbor right below his apartment was a friend of my dad's and started calling me every few days, then every other day, then every day.

"Your dad fell again," he would say. "So, I went upstairs to help him."

One day, the call came but this time he was angry. "Your dad fell and you need to get here. I'm not doing this anymore. You know your dad keeps falling and the thump is loud and he's going to get hurt.".

He was right, we needed to do something. But right before the falling started, we had already started adjusting things around the apartment, trying everything we could to keep Dad in his home because he loved it so much: his friends, the view of the river, Charlie and me down the street...

We already equipped the bathroom with new-everything such as multiple rails and a commode, so our next adjustment was adding a living room recliner. Something about the chair's deep brown, shiny "pleather" somehow helped Dad glide right onto his walker: part flying machine, part air lift, part ejection seat, it worked. For a while, anyway. Until Dad became afraid of the 'air lift' factor, and well, he stopped sitting in the chair.

Next, we decided to give the sofa a try. (No slippery fake leather, just cloth.) But there was one problem; it was too low.

My husband Charlie, problem-solver-extraordinaire and master carpenter, always has a solution for everything. Dad said, "Charlie, can you do something about this?" Lo and behold, Charlie made custom wood blocks to fit each leg of the sofa to raise it six inches. And it worked. (Of course it did. Charlie made them.) Dad was so happy. (Okay. Another problem solved.)

Next was the bed. "Charlie, I'm having a hard time getting out of bed."

Charlie thought about it, "All right, Len, I will come up with a solution."

Since we didn't have access to an expensive hospital bed with all the electronic gadgets built into it (or how we'd even get one into the elevator, let alone, through the doorways and into his room,) of course Charlie came up with another solution. He devised a pulley system that worked for a while, until Dad didn't have the strength to even hold onto the pulley anymore.

Pulley system now obsolete, Dad couldn't get to the bathroom anymore, so we tried a commode next to the bed, but he was losing strength and couldn't get out of bed to get to that, now, either. I couldn't run over there every hour to assist with everything, so now we had a decision to make, and it wasn't going to be easy. He officially needed "care." A heartbreaking development.

I had *promised* my dad that I would never put him in a nursing home. But we had no choice, and our little team knew it.

It was a dark day I will never forget when Charlie and I went to see Dad to give him the news. At this point, it had only been a couple of days that Dad couldn't do anything outside of being in bed, but that was already too long, especially since we could hardly get him to the bathroom.

So, Dad's there trapped in bed while Charlie and I are in the room struggling to get the words out regarding what had to happen.

All three of us cried and cried. I felt the most disappointed in myself I had been up to that point in my life. This was it. Doom was upon us. Next stop: Nursing home.

Write a NEW Post-it note (or 2, or 3, or 4...)

I'm beautiful!
I've got this.
I'm doing great!
I'm AMAZING.
Keep going,
Give Love, Get LOVE!

Stick them around the Mirror
of the bathroom you use every day.

Budget & Finances

Emotional distress doesn't understand money. Rich or poor, having your entire emotional body wrapped up in your parent's life is difficult, regardless of whether you have means, or how much help you have. True, some have the money to hire private nurses to provide around-the-clock care for their mom or dad, but even that luxury doesn't mean they don't carry physical and emotional burdens. No one is exempt from the pain of someone that is in nursing care, whether at home or in a facility. Don't be hard on yourself. Or them.

Everyone in these situations needs help and no one can blame anyone for taking full advantage of all options available to them.

Follow The Money - Nothing Is Impossible
By the time Dad had to go to a nursing home, we had exhausted his savings. Thankfully, Dad qualified for Medicaid and his social security covered his nursing home stay, but when I look back, I realize there was a better way. We later found out he could have qualified to either get money to help pay his bills or possibly have them exempted, but figuring out care facility financials takes a considerable effort to coordinate and a lot of time to research and make calls. By then my workload already had me on auto-pilot with neither time nor energy to spare.

Instead, I set a goal to find a nursing home that would work with what we had. I wouldn't take NO for an answer.

Having a career in the Arts means pushing, hustling, getting rejected more times than I care to count, so owning a natural determination helps push through rejection to only focus on the "acceptance," the YES: the *Yes, you've got this. Yes, you can do this.* The *YES you can*!

Dad was falling all the time in his own apartment and was unable to lift himself out of bed or get to the bathroom, so we finally accepted he needed 24-hour care. At this stage, there are two choices, and sometimes only one, depending on your budget:

1. Private nurses (that come to the house if you can afford to do so.)
2. A nursing care facility.

Unfortunately, the first choice wasn't an option, so we needed to find a suitable nursing home.

Living in rural Pennsylvania, our choices were fewer than ideal. We looked at every single available option from the very limited list—especially since my dad needed to be in a facility that accepted Medicaid. (The so-called *better* nursing care facilities only accept a certain number of Medicaid recipients to live at their homes, so those slots are typically full or waitlisted.) But I decided right then and there I would not take NO for an answer.

Some of the nursing home options were so depressing, my heart exploded with anger; so we ultimately settled on an unimpressive facility that was close to our home where at least I could visit every day.

And when I say "settled", unfortunately I mean it. At first the place seemed 'okay,' 'good enough,' I thought. I could supplement with my own caregiving by showing up a few times a day, calling frequently, and so forth. Boy was I wrong. The place was bad. It was only a couple of weeks in that the trashy staff and employees proved the writing was on the wall (which turned into a couple of months while we tried in desperation to relocate him.)

Thinking it was the staff at first, I tried bringing the caregivers bagels, donuts, pizza and so forth, to soften them up, thinking maybe the aids and nurses would give better care to Dad because of the gifts.

Did they work? I don't think so.

Day by day, Dad got more and more depressed just being there. We tried to make the best of it but the heavy, dark energy of the place created no feeling of home. My dad even reported that "one of the aids jumps on his bed." He said, "I'm scared. I'm scared I might fall off the bed! She thinks it's funny!"

I left that day and cried. It officially wasn't a good fit. A real *What am I going to do?*

Meanwhile, my father always gave the best advice—I don't care whether from bed, or a chair, or land, or sea… he was my dad, my rock, the rock of Gibraltar—the best and strongest man in the world. So, the next day, I just came out and asked him point blank:

"Dad, I don't know what to do. What should I do to help you?"

I will never forget what he said. He was crying.

"I want to go back to New York. I just want to go back to New York and die there".

We were both crying now: "Okay." I hugged him. "Okay, Dad. I will get you back to New York."

New York was now his last dying wish.

I thought, *OK! I'll just make a phone call and Voila! Back to NYC. Get Dad in a nursing home on Long Island where my brother lives and he can give care to Dad the rest of Dad's life. Great.*

Little did I know how difficult, wait—make that *how incredibly difficult* that was going to be. But remember the part about not taking No for an answer? Thankfully, I have tough skin. (OK, well, sort of... maybe...) Anyway, I do believe we are only given what we can handle, so I thought *here goes nothing!*

I started by calling a nursing facility on Long Island and explaining my dad is living in Pennsylvania on Medicaid and I need to find him a place in New York. The response: *What? Never heard of that. What do you mean? You can't move someone state to state on Medicaid!*

"You mean to tell me you've *never* done it?"

That's right because it can't be done.

"Okay. Thank you." I hung up, figuring that was just one facility. Until, I called around everywhere. I wrote and researched for three straight weeks. Call after call, e-mail after e-mail, absolutely everyone told me *hard NO! NO, NO, NO! Can't do it, can't do it. No. NO. And NO!*

Still, I said to myself *YES! I will make this happen. I AM going to make this work for him*...Then I'd be back on the phone, pleading, voice crackling and tears rolling down my face with every single call. I just needed to find one person with a sympathetic heart... compassion... ANYTHING:

> *But he was born and raised in New York. He actually lived there his entire life except for four short years in Pennsylvania with us. He wants to die in New York! How come no one is listening to me?*

Most said, "Oh I'm sorry, but I can't help you." But sorry wasn't enough. I was determined to make it happen, so I decided to go to Long Island and meet with these heartless humans face-to-face. After all, I also grew up in New York and these essentially were my people, right?

Next began the actual journey. Thankfully my closest and dearest friend, Cindy, also the sweetest and kindest human, offered to take me around to all the nursing home facilities. We traveled to each home and talked to them without bringing up the situation. If we liked a place, I'd ease into asking, "Do you have room to take a Medicaid recipient?"

If they said yes, I would share the story of how we were moving him from Pennsylvania to New York, and the clockwork responses would come: "Oh, NO, we can't do that!"

Each facility the same: day one, then day two, then day three, until...

On the *third* day of visits (and too many tears to count,) Cindy had an idea:

"You remember so and so, my neighbor?" (I did.) "He was at a nursing home that worked out well. He received good care and liked it there. It's not that far away..."

I don't know why she hadn't thought of it sooner, but worn out from trying to make sense of everything going on plus just thinking about the task of moving dad whenever we did find a solution, and... and... I wanted to scream. So Cindy's suggestion was my last hope. That third day, we went to Meadowbrook Care Center and met with the administrator.

After a lot of chatter (and all the hope in my heart,) the administrator finally said, "We can do it."

She. Said. YES!

Meadowbrook would be Dad's final home. I would be able to grant his dying wish!

***

While my exact circumstances may differ from yours, you likely agree we will each fight the good fight to do whatever needs to happen in order for us to grant our parent their last wishes.

> ## A Caregiver's Perspective: Erin
>
> Both my parents were sole proprietors, so things immediately got out of control financially for my family once Dad got sick. My dad, a small business owner, couldn't work through it— you don't get sick pay when you have your own business. My mom also couldn't take time off at her own business, as she had to keep it going just to pay the health insurance, $1500/ month alone, on top of all the other bills.
>
> Back then, health insurance had no cost protections in place, so the insurer kept raising the insurance rates every other month. We paid more in monthly insurance for Dad's expenses than my mom's monthly salary. Plus, they didn't have a pancreatic cancer specialist here in the desert, so he was being treated in Los Angeles. That meant on top of everything else, his treatments required commuting to LA—almost two hours without traffic. Add gas plus a $100/ day for parking at the hospital? It was bankrupting my parents.

At that point, Mom and I became full-time caregivers. She saw clients during the day when I would be Dad's caregiver, and I took a night job nannying so Mom could take over Dad's care. Dad's chance of survival was less than 3%, so we wanted to be with him as much as possible.

Never UNDERESTIMATE what you can do.

Advocacy

Advocate: noun; intransitive verb
A person who publicly supports or recommends a particular cause or policy.
–Oxford Dictionary
To act as advocate for someone or something. –Merriam Webster
A tradition of advocating for the equality and civil rights of all people.
–Fred Kuhr

Preparing to be the Advocate

Until I became Dad's caregiver, I had no idea what being an advocate for another person was or how to do it. Once my father started going in and out of the hospital, a very kind nurse (there are lots of them), instructed me, "You need to be your Dad's advocate."

Then I came to understand what this meant: the minute you become a caregiver for your parent you are their advocate, especially the more regularly the medical community is involved in your parent's routines.

I thought I was already doing this by taking him to doctor and chemo appointments, keeping his diet and nutrition in check, caring for his home/ laundry/ shopping/ bills, and managing his overall well-being. However, advocacy means you provide your voice to protect them, make sure their wishes are granted, and what's most important, keep them safe.

A Caregiver's Perspective: Lexie

I was with both my mom and my dad during every doctor appointment, so I had my finger on the pulse. I knew what was going on with their medical stuff. I had separate notebooks where I would write everything

> down to keep track. It was huge that I knew the medication my mom was taking. Doctors pay attention when you are the Advocate.

Medications

As an advocate, you *need* to know every medication your parent is taking.

Isn't that a concern for their doctor? Yes and no.

Yes, doctors will prescribe medications and you need to make sure your parent takes them at the appropriate time for them to work properly. Just keep in mind, it's awful to need so much medication, and worse to become forgetful as a side effect of taking so much medication. Part of keeping Mom or Dad safe is to know exactly what medications they are taking, and when (actual times of day) plus cumulatively *how often* (rough totals) each day or week to track potential issues—even just the names if each one's purpose is too confusing to memorize.

Refer to this information whenever you take your parent to a doctor, especially with multiple doctors in the mix. Start with their primary care doctor. Next, if your parent is in a nursing home, get friendly with their nurse, (every resident is assigned a nurse at the facility.) If your Mom or Dad is at the hospital instead, be sure to check that the actual medications they take when back home or in the nursing care facility *match* the medications they are receiving at the hospital—that they are the same. This is frequently not the case.

Details as this seem to get lost along the way yet this is a very important part of being an advocate. Inevitably there will be a time when your parent can't remember what pills to take, when, or how many, so this is one of your jobs. **Keep track of the medications.**

If remembering is too much for you, at the very least, help them get organized by writing out the details or taking pictures with your phone and making copies to be easily accessed via cell phone, email, or even hard copies to be removed from their purse or wallet and shared as the need arises.

A Caregiver's Perspective: Amber

When my mom came home to the apartment from the care facility, I looked at all the new medications she was on instead of the original two when she first went there. Now there were six. As a result, she was drowsy a lot.

One day she fell while I was actually standing right next to her. But I had to be careful about the way I grabbed her while falling as I didn't want to make it worse, so she fell on the coffee table and hit her ear. I took her to the ER and she got two stitches.

Once I took her back to her regular nurse practitioner and primary care doctor, mom went back to only being on two medications. One manages cognitive function and the other is an anti- depressant. I got my mom back to a degree, as she wasn't as slumberous once her medications changed again.

Pill boxes with the days of the week imprinted on them are a popular favorite amongst seniors because overwhelmed persons forget what pills to take each day and how many. My Dad knew his pills by color and shape. He would say "Now I take the two pink ovals." (I always found it funny that his memory never failed; it was his body that didn't cooperate.)

We were more relaxed once I got him his pill box. Even if he did remember everything on his own, there are always days when he wasn't feeling great. Those are the times your parent is most likely to forget. (Remember: keep them safe!) On that note, make sure you are the one that consistently sets the pill box up each week to simplify accountability and tracking.

When you purchase your pill box at the drug store (or order online,) spend the extra couple of dollars for these options if you can:

- *Weekly format*, to ensure the week's medication gets taken properly and so anyone on your team can step in to handle this very important task if needed.
- *Opens easily*, as some tend to stick and become another frustration.
- *Appropriate size* for how many pills Mom or Dad take each day.

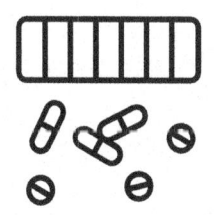

A Caregiver's Perspective: Val

My mom left notes everywhere. I still have one on my mirror:

*"Dear Valerie,
You are such a blessing, so loving and caring,
I thank God for you always. Love, Mom."*

---

*You want to do this: You want to be their caregiver.
Let them know.
Tell them you love them often—even daily.*

Dignity & Deep Listening

There was a time I thought to myself, *how can Dad want to live? He is really suffering and is so sick. This doesn't make sense to me. Why? How?*

I really didn't enjoy having these thoughts, but you may also have them. This is a normal reaction when you see someone suffering daily. *How can they possibly want this? What quality of life is this? Will my amazing Dad be able to maintain his dignity?*

Two ER doctors in the hospital in Pennsylvania used that word twice on two separate occasions: "Your dad is very sick. I don't think he will make it through the night. And I want this man to maintain his dignity."

Honestly, I wasn't sure what that meant: maintain his *dignity*? So, were their decisions the doctors' wishes or the wish of the man whose life was in their hands?

Both times, we had to face the reality he may die—("tonight"), and both times I remember crying harder than I ever thought was possible and staying at the hospital as long as we could. We went home very late to get a few hours of sleep, understanding Dad may not make it through either night. Both times Dad was so sick and so weak, I thought how could he possibly make it through and then recover?

Lo and behold, he made it through. Both times (with his dignity in tact.) And he even lived three more years in New York.

Life is really unpredictable. Look at your own life: what things have you thought were going one way, then went in the totally opposite direction? It seems the more we push an idea thinking our life will go a certain way, the more it fools us into going another direction. There is a saying: "Plan all you want, although the outcome may not be what you expect."

As a result, I have learned to **listen**. Listen to what your mom or dad wants, and what they have to say. It's valuable. It's important. Remember that what you may want for them and what they may want for themselves may be two totally different things. If your parent can still make decisions, you really need to honor them. Only when they can't do you become the sole decision-maker. This was the BIGGEST and the hardest lesson I have ever learned in my life: Listen to them. And I do not take that lightly.

While I was his caregiver, I had to learn how to step back and be more of an observer. Toward the end when he was so sick, in and out of the hospital, I stopped thinking, how is *he still living through this Hell*? I learned to allow him to live out his life

'Lenny- style': granting him more control over his decisions. This was extremely difficult, although the more I leaned into it, the more joy he found.

I mean, who was I to judge how another person's life should unfold? Or what his struggles and joy should be?

If you can fully relax while being your parents advocate, it's a beautiful experience to witness. It's not easy. You must learn to expand how much you can let go and let live. I learned my own interpretation of what "living with dignity" meant instead of those ER doctors' version. It meant helping a man who wanted to live, live his life, whether from a bustling city apartment or only the view from his bed in each moment... hour... day... month... or one year at a time.

They say the end of life is a reflection of our beginning.

Dad's ending was mirroring his beginning, (maybe even his life as a whole?) I heard the same thing almost daily through my caregiving days: "Lenny was a gentleman and one of the kindest individuals I have ever known." "Your father is the nicest person." "Your father is so genuine." "Your father always asks me how I am doing." "Your father doesn't complain." *Your father, your father...* Every time someone started a sentence "Your father," I knew exactly what was going to follow. I could finish their sentences, *yup... the nicest, kindest, most genuine person?*

Did that make caregiving easier? Sure. Not always, although it helped. This was to be the sum of his short 80 years of existence here on earth. This and being the greatest man in the world...

Lenny's Story

My first-generation Italian father, Leonard Salvatore LaCoppola (Lenny,) was a handsome devil: olive skin, light brown complexion, with a full head of kinky, curly jet-black hair. He grew up the second youngest of nine kids in a railroad apartment in Harlem, New York City. It was tight quarters with nine kids plus two adults in a two-bedroom flat—that is, until my father's quite-older siblings began to move out one-by-one over time.

When we were kids, Lenny would slave over the stove all day making spaghetti and meatballs for the big Sunday family dinner. We all sat around the big table and Dad would always tell stories of growing up in Harlem... playing dice under the stairs. Jumping subway turnstiles to deliver "things" dropped from windows uptown that he'd have to catch in both hands while standing on the sidewalk without letting them hit the ground before rushing to take them on the subway somewhere downtown...

He told stories of how he snuck into Manhattan's movie theaters as a boy, (the back door, of course.) He'd make friends with the guy selling the popcorn who snuck him and his friends in to see the double features. Sometimes during the hot, hazy, humid summers, they would spend all day at the movies just to stay cool in the free A/C.

Some stories sounded tall; others just plain rough and tumble—things I couldn't imagine. I know he had a hard time as a kid: nine kids in a railroad apartment in New York City with a father who spoke Italian and very little broken English. Dad always said he could count on two hands how many times his father spoke to him as a kid, the most frequent being "Children are seen but not heard."

He had a rough time as a child with good and bad memories, lots of struggle, although I believe lots of love too. When Dad's mother passed away at age 15, he was sent to Long Island, New York, to live with his older sister, Cecelia, and her husband, Donald.

Ceil and Don had a big house with horses next door, quite the change from city life. I think Dad missed the city's excitement and the Manhattan Boys and Girls Club where Dad was a table tennis champion throughout the Burroughs. That and swimming in the indoor pool which kept him out of trouble, away from the Italian mob that was always in search of new recruits. He said there wasn't enough to do as a teenager in Long Island where the kids he knew liked to drink too much—not his idea of fun.

And let me tell you a secret. What I'm about to say, well, (just imagine I've put my hands around your ear and am whispering, *Shhhh, you can't tell anyone… the guilt!*) Dad was my favorite parent.

I mean, I waited nightly for him to come home from work—sometimes until 10 p.m. when he'd drag himself through the door and I would scramble to the oven removing his food and telling him, "Sit down and let me get you some dinner."

He worked hard, too hard, and physical labor takes its toll. At the end he was tired, exhausted really. His whole body was collapsing after too many jobs, too much work, mostly in the moving business. Even after he had his own trucks and ran his own business, he still worked physically, packing up box after box in the New York public's homes. (That's also why we never knew quite what time he'd get home.)

Once he became bedbound he used to say, "I'm just so tired. I pushed myself too much. I need rest, I need rest."

Even though Dad lost control of his body, his mind remained

sharp as a tack. He remembered everything. In spite of staying in bed full-time, he still had opinions and ideas. He was living in his head and wanted to live (most of the time.) He accepted that his view of life was from bed now, and enjoyed living anyway, enjoyed the moments. He loved to meet new people, loved to eat his favorite foods, read books, watch movies—he LOVED movies. He remembered every actor and film title, especially ones from the past.

But we'll hit pause on Lenny's story. We have more living, loving and caregiving to cover...

This will not last FOREVER.
Take a breath.
Repeat your mantras.
You've GOT THIS!

Nursing Home
& Care Facilities

A Caregiver's Perspective: Tyler

The next phase for Mom was finding a senior memory care center. We found one pretty close to my sister's house: a day center that specifically catered to seniors with memory problems, AND it was covered 100% by her insurance.

The van came Monday through Friday and drove her to the center. She spent the whole day there and came home around 4 p.m. Mom liked it. She was young compared to a lot of the participants there, so it was a really cool thing for her. She felt ahead of the game since she still had her memory, and her body was functioning normally.

After a few years, waking up and getting ready started becoming a problem for my mom. She couldn't do basic things on her own any longer. We got approved for a certain number of in-home support hours through her insurance and found a caring woman to help her in the mornings with showers and getting ready for the program. That same person came back at night and got Mom ready for bed.

This was an amazing resource which helped for a while, but it wasn't sustainable. Mom was getting worse. Yet my sisters and I were determined to keep her at home as long as we possibly could. We honestly thought we could keep her there forever. Unfortunately, that wasn't going to work.

So, we went on a hunt for homes and facilities. We visited state facilities—absolutely disgusting, a definite No. Yes, they are the cheapest facilities, although there is a reason.

Unfortunately, rent at most of the competent places is about $4000/ month and up, (and $4000 is on the very low end of things.) Once the patient adds a memory care issue, the price goes up. This makes it super-expensive for families. It's why so many try to keep their loved ones at home for as long as possible; they can't afford facility care.

We finally found a great place for mom only about 40 minutes from all of us: a small family-owned facility with only 16 beds. The family lives on the backside of the property. It's comforting because it looks similar to a home, and being family-owned, it has a great staff. We now pay $1500/ month for my mom's facility, and her social security pays the rest. My mom has Medicaid to cover medications and Depends (adult diapers)—basic supplies—but that's all it covers.

Naturally there was an adjustment period. In the beginning she would say "I want to go home! I want to go home!" But after three years, she's good now. She's still walking, talking, singing and hanging strong! She gets the best care. Anytime she needs anything, or something happens, we are called right away.

As you're discovering, finding a care facility such as a nursing home may be time-consuming, frustrating, and sometimes disappointing. You're emotionally drained and you just want what's best for your parent. It's a much more difficult task if you're paying out of pocket or working around Medicaid restrictions. So put your best foot forward and march into this with an open mind, while also looking for clues and signs of unfavorable institutions.

I accept that working at a care facility is a taxing job, but some of the administrators need to have a gentler approach and be more accommodating. Then again, others are just plain awesome, and I realize some conditions may be out of their control.

The Staff

The Aides & The Nurses

First, you want to make sure you learn the Nurses and Aides assigned to your parent. Most of the time at 24/7 operational facilities, there is a daytime nurse plus an aide, then a nighttime pair. There may also be aides and nurses that fill in on days off, so introduce yourself to all these facilitators as soon as you can.

Let the nurses know that you are available anytime to talk about your parent and their needs. You are here for them to make everything go smoothly. Ask the nurses, *how may I assist you?*

Bringing food or gifts to the staff goes a long way for goodwill. We brought items such as two dozen bagels with tubs of butter and cream cheese, or donuts, cookies, themed holiday candy, etc.. Aides and nurses work long hours and love little surprises and treats that make their day (or week.) They will talk about it all the time and will thank your parent as well.

Facility Evaluation Criteria

Pay attention to these signs:

- ✦ If it smells strongly, stay away. (Note that all facilities have a *little* odor.)
- ✦ Is it clean? Do you see staff cleaning on your visit?
- ✦ How many residents are in the hallways in wheelchairs at one time?
- ✦ Do the residents all look heavily sedated?
- ✦ Are the staff friendly when you visit?
- ✦ Is the place bright with lots of windows?
- ✦ Do the rooms have enough space? There should only be a maximum of two residents per room. If there are more than that; walk away, the facility is not operating in this century.
- ✦ Did you check reviews? They will all have some negative reviews, (emotions trigger reactions,) but mentions of "elder abuse" are the red flag. Look over the "average" reviews a little more deeply, too: do those reviews contain positives between the lines?

My research turned up additional questions to ask nursing homes, too. The first one about turnover for nurse's aides is important, as they really are the backbone of a care facility. Some of Meadowbrook's nurse's aides had been there for over twenty years—and it showed because they noticeably nurtured the residents (and of course, loved my dad). Additionally, the medical director had served the center for many years.

More criteria:

- ✦ What is the turnover rate for nurse's aides?
- ✦ How long has the Medical Director been at the facility?
- ✦ What is the reputation of the nursing staff?
- ✦ What is the status of the facility's recreation and social services?

Finally, you may ask if the facility is accredited, but accreditation is not a deal breaker. Accreditation shows that the facility has taken extra steps to comply with The Joint Commission, (formerly known as the Joint Commission on Accreditation of Hospitals or JCOAH.) It is a strictly voluntary step, nevertheless, it shows that they've taken that extra step, so only a handful of nursing homes are deemed accredited.

Source: Baylor University

Food

Food is our connection to life, to our family and friends. It literally sustains us, brings us pleasure and joy. There is nothing better than sharing a meal with loved ones. My dad always said he hated to eat alone, so I tried as best I could to have as many meals with him as possible. Life is so full of precious moments, shared meals being amongst the most wonderful way to create memories.

When it comes to food in care facilities, your parent may not get all the nutrition or culinary delights they want, so bring them food that you make or order them food from a local restaurant and have it delivered. We had food delivered to Dad all the time, especially from his favorite pizza place on Fridays. (I always included a big tip for the delivery guy, as he delivered the food right to Dad's room, helped Dad un-bag the food and even opened his favorite bottle of root beer. Acknowledge the kind souls in the world by paying them for their services.)

Don't forget to cook extra food from your own meals so you can share it with Mom or Dad when you visit. Having been immobile most of his time in the nursing home, Dad really looked forward to sharing in the edible treats my brother, Angelo, and I would bring him, as well as whatever else any other visitors brought him. Even so, making our parents happy with simple treats like foods they enjoy in turn brings us happiness.
Care facilities tend to make a lot of the same foods, the same way. Be very specific when asking how much they will work with you regarding what food Mom or Dad likes to eat, and how they prefer things prepared. Keep it simple. For example, Dad loved to eat roasted chicken along with a baked potato and salad, often eating this a few days a week.

When my dad really wasn't feeling well, getting closer to dying, we met with the nutritionist. I commented how the food my dad preferred lately wasn't as healthy and perhaps he wasn't making the best choices anymore. The nutritionist looked at me squarely and said, "It's okay. Let Lenny have what he wants."

I understood. I took her advice as if to say, *It doesn't matter anymore, Debra. Let the man enjoy*, and immediately remembered the lesson about letting Dad make his own decisions. It was as if I had amnesia. So, I took a moment of silence with a lump in my throat and a tear in my eye. I also see now; I was in denial about losing my father. We get so involved in their life, we think this 'maintenance stage' will last forever and that we will continue to keep fixing everything. (Maybe you can relate? I've since learned it's a subtle form of denial.)

If your parent is really sick and nearing the end, it's okay, let them indulge. The larger facilities have gift and/or coffee shops that may offer free ice cream for residents. Ours allowed up to one scoop per day—a definite plus. (Who doesn't love ice cream?) And they usually have a sherbet if Mom or Dad need to go dairy-free.

Intuition & Gut Feelings

Trust Yours

Remember, you are your parent's advocate. Doctors are overwhelmed. Sometimes you need to do your homework. You need to check with the doctors and nurses and make sure Mom or Dad is getting the right medications. Again, get to know that nurse they are assigned to and introduce yourself to all the key contacts involved in your parent's care so when things come up, you don't feel lost trying to figure out who to speak with. There are always so many things to stay on top of even when they are in a nursing care facility.

For example, I knew every time my dad had a UTI way before the nursing home. Dad and I had a close relationship. We spoke every day, sometimes 2-3 times a day if he needed to talk. His body may have been giving out the last few years of his life, but his mind never left us, (as sharp as a tack, remember?) The minute Dad got confused or skipped asking basics, *what we were having for dinner that night*, or *how our home renovation was going*, I knew he had a UTI and should be checked for hydration.

The nursing home staff never understood how I knew. It's because caregiving to someone you deeply love means you really know them, as well as you know yourself, sometimes better. It's also why having one main point person as caregiver is so important: the upside is someone focused on every detail of their life to catch the little variances.

Yes, it's still essential to have a team (we reviewed in *building your squad* chapter.) It's also essential to have one main Advocate, and that is you. It's a big responsibility, although with the right help and support, you will do amazing work.

> ### A Caregiver's Perspective: Amber
>
> I have always had a background in retail and customer service, which taught me how to connect with people. Yes, as an esthetician, clients want their brows done or their facial, however, I've learned what they actually value and pay you for is your time.
>
> This is their way of de-stressing, their way of doing self-care. So, I learned to actively listen and how to interject constructively into conversation. I didn't realize how important those skills (as well as being intuitive to a degree) would help me as a caregiver.

You know what to do:
Use your instinct and trust your intuition.

The Hospital

A Caregiver's Perspective: Val

My Mother began to repeatedly tell us:
"You don't understand, I am tired. My body is old and I can't do the things I used to do."

Hospital Nurse Relations

Hospitals differ from care facilities. Every time Mom or Dad goes into the hospital, you must find the nurse on the first day you visit. Get to know each one that comes in on every shift you're there. Introduce yourself and let them know you are your parent's caregiver and advocate.

How to work with them.
Nurses are (usually) really awesome. Become friends with them. Let them know YOU care, as it helps them to care more. With the new COVID reality comes a shortage of nurses. Nurses are stressed-out more than ever. Many left the profession entirely because of burnout and stress. Now traveling nurses are a 'thing.' They come from all over the country (and world) to assist many hospitals across the nation based on need. As a result, nurses appreciate all the support they can get. (Just as with teachers and children, it's not the nurses role to manage your parent's well-being, solo.)

It is even more important to make yourself visible and available to all the nurses on their shifts. They will come to rely on you as their patient's advocate, so get involved in your parent's hospital stay and try to be as vocal as possible. Above all, however, Be Kind. They have been stretched to the limit of their profession.

Nurses either work the day shift or the night shift. The night shift typically starts at 3:00 p.m. or 4:00 p.m. Your goal is to connect with nurses on both day and night shifts, and anyone else filling in when possible. Keep in mind that nurses switch shifts and sometimes switch patients too, (I hope infrequently for your parent's circumstances, as this does complicate matters.) I have recited my dad's history, needs, and status more times than I can count. I know it sounds strange, but if you are new to this, it gets exhausting. I learned through trial and error and I am sharing the highlights so you can skip most of the 'error' part.

This is what nurses & staff appreciate from you:

- Very important: make sure they have your **CORRECT** phone number. Have them repeat it back! Numbers get mixed up so you may never get calls intended to provide updates or ask questions. I've had this happen and I don't want it to happen to you.

- Also verify face-to-face they have all the **CORRECT** emergency contact information. If more contacts are on the list than you, make sure everyone's correct. Hospital records are rarely reliable.

- The third basic to cover is whether your parent has **ALLERGIES**—to medications or food. Absolutely make sure this is known as well. The nursing home and the hospital don't communicate well so it's up to you to make sure what works in the nursing home works in the hospital.

- **Anxiety meds or other pills:** Unfortunately, I can't even count how many times my dear Dad had to go to the hospital, and every time it was heart-wrenching. I always knew he wasn't feeling mentally well in the hospital. I would check on his medications and every single time without fail, I could tell they weren't giving it to him.

(I mean, you're sick, bedbound, and now you're in the hospital: wouldn't you want to have your anxiety medication to help take the edge off?) I would ask the nurse to make sure he was getting his anxiety medication and they would always reply that the anxiety meds had to be authorized by the doctor.

(Mind you, something already prescribed by a doctor that he took every day as part of his standard medications.)

I would ask *how* is this *different*? launching the same routine: hospital calls nursing home, tells nursing home to call the hospital back, and the cycle began. My father always waited up to 48 hours later for his anxiety medication as the doctors never got back to the nurses to get back to the hospital nurses in a timely way. It's a horrible system: frustrating, infuriating, and part of being your parent's advocate.

Meanwhile, **you must still be considerate to everyone at the hospital!** They are taking care of your parent: the nurses, cleaning crew, employees that deliver their food, everyone… No matter how angry or frustrated you are, smile, say hello, ask them how their day is going, and say thank you. Sometimes it's awkward, although the truth is, you don't want even subconscious aggression or worse, retaliation, to play out during your parent's care.

Thankfully, my dad was super friendly. We always said he could make friends in an elevator. (I literally watched it once: they got coffee together following the ride!) Regardless, you can't rely on your parent's good nature to diffuse tension you just created with the hospital staff.

Also be kind to the other patient(s) sharing the room with your parent. These days it is very rare your parent will have a room to themselves, unless they have a contagious disease. Translation:

they will have a roommate. My dad befriended just about every hospital roommate he had, unless, of course, they couldn't talk. Then he would befriend their visitors instead. Sometimes those visitors asked Dad if he wanted coffee or food, so I always did the same in return.

Engaging Hospital Roommates & Their Visitors:

- ✛ If you're getting food for your parent: ask the roommate if they want something.
- ✛ If you're going to a store: ask the roommate if they need anything. (Most of the time they say no, but at least you asked, and in turn, others may do the same for your loved one.)
- ✛ Let the roommate know you care. Ask them how they're feeling today. (Your parent will have an easier time with that person and their visitors will do the same.)

I realize these are simple suggestions, yet anything that eases stress makes caregiving easier.

Hospital HR & Finance Departments

How to work with them...

Dad's finances weren't in great shape, mostly attributable to paying all his medical bills in full before realizing he could be getting assistance. Money is another place caregivers help.

At first, I lacked awareness of the resources that were out there. I was using all his money to pay his medical bills—his *retirement*, his *savings*! He was living with us, and the bills kept coming, so I kept paying. I called the collectors, the hospitals, the surgeons, the doctors, the specialists and plead with them, *this is all the money he has...* And NOT ONCE, NOT. ONCE. did anyone say, "you may qualify for assistance."

When you're frenzied in new territory, you're not yourself. You just can't see things the way you normally would. In any other circumstance, I would have found this information out sooner, but my emotions had taken over and I was focused on making sure my dad was going to survive the care part. Navigating unknown territory may feel as though you're at war with everyone.

So, during one of Dad's hospital stays, I decided to see the social worker. The social worker connected me to HR. I went to HR and that was it: I finally met an ANGEL who helped me. She walked me through the steps to get assistance. I cried. She consoled. It just takes ONE person to reach their hand out to help you so, the biggest lesson is: ***If you don't ask for help, nobody knows you need assistance.***

Once others know you need help they often step up. The challenge is to ask a lot of the public. I used to approach the same three individuals and now realize it takes asking ten, twenty, or more. Why stop? You don't need to isolate to friends and family. People rise to the occasion to help.

So, the takeaway is:
Please ask for help at every turn, during every stage.

Honestly, I had supportive persons in my life, but I was so overwhelmed doing everything that I didn't even know *what* to ask anyone. How to address/ who to address/ and which one to ask for *what*? Your support team should help you navigate these things. At the hospital that means nurses and administration, elsewhere there are other key players.

First,

If your parent is on Medicaid or insurance, reach out to the HR department and the Finance department for help navigating this arena. Ask:

- ✦ what is covered by insurance,
- ✦ what is out of pocket,
- ✦ and what types of assistance you can get.

Next,

Connect with the Social Worker at the hospital. It shows that you care about what is happening with your parent. In addition to staying on top of things, you are your parent's advocate and these new contacts become your advocate. At the very least you will have more information than you started with.

Stop and take 5 minutes (set a timer.)
Sit in a chair with your feet on the floor.
Close your eyes.
Imagine yourself in your favorite natural setting:
the beach, the forest, an English garden...
Really try to see yourself there.
Now feel your shoulders sink away from your ears.
Be mindful of your jaw: Relax your jaw.
Now relax your face.
Now just breathe for as long as it takes.
You are loved.

Directives + Living Will

Importance of...
This is a hard ask, nevertheless you will be asked, and you will need to be clear what Mom's or Dad's wishes are regarding resuscitation, ventilation, and possibly other procedural options. Resuscitation and ventilation were the two most important to us, and those subjects are the opposite of easy conversations to have. But they are necessary and require advance planning, so you're not caught in a terrible spot making decisions when you're emotional and possibly alone.

We put these details in place with Dad's very first surgery. Although it wasn't a life-threatening procedure, it was a good opening. These documents need to be notarized, so if your parent can't make it to the office of a notary, look up a mobile notary who can come to you do all the paperwork on-the-spot. They are less expensive than they sound. Every time my dad went into the hospital, I verified that our directives were in place. It's hard enough to see them suffer. The last thing you want is more problems.

Remember, you are your parent's advocate. Your job is to make sure they are safe and protected.

After the hospital directives come the many options once Mom or Dad pass. It is hard to think about, nevertheless, trust me, it's harder once it happens. Most post-mortem arrangements should already be in place. This is part of self-caring, too. It is so overwhelming when our parent passes that having to remember what their wishes are while trying to process grief is not healthy. It is best to have your parents write a will specifying their wishes for leaving Earth.

Many years ago, my parents bought burial plots next to my grandparents. Thankfully, my dad also had life insurance which would pay for the funeral arrangements we lined up. But we still needed to make some decisions once Dad passed, so I was grateful almost everything was in place already. Take it from me, arrange as much as you can.

> ### A Caregiver's Perspective: Lexie
>
> Because doctors want to keep patients alive, some doctors won't want to put your parent in hospice. It's as if the doctors don't want to acknowledge that your parent is not going to live. Please understand, hospice is the patient's right!
>
> My only regret with Dad's dying process was not having hospice. My Dad's last three months of life would have been different if we had hospice. It would have made our whole experience with his death and dying so much more balanced and supportive. The doctor really steered us away from this.
>
> I must have asked him a half dozen times, "isn't it time to get George, (my dad,) into hospice?"
>
> And the doctor kept saying "NO."

A Caregiver's Perspective: Amber

My parents never made a will, but at least we discussed their medical wishes and what they wanted at their time of death. We had life insurance policies in place, although we never talked about what could happen with long-term care. I don't know if this [avoidance] is generational or cultural, but this topic has been really hard for me.

A Caregiver's Perspective: Dr. Penelope

My mother was up at night going through every little item, which wasn't much at that stage in her life. For example, a picture on the wall—a beautiful little painting of daffodils which had come from someone special. I'd quietly tear off a piece of masking tape, shhhhh, then Mom would put somebody's name on it and placed it on the back of each belonging.

Everything was given away after the first month. She had made her disposition.

> ### A Caregiver's Perspective: Val
>
> My parents had already bought everything for their funerals, although at some point during her final stages, my mother began to write note after note telling us, "I want to be cremated." She placed these notes around the house.
>
> When I asked her about it, she said, "I changed my mind. I know I said I wanted a casket before, but I want to be cremated now."

Hospital Food

Managing & Supplementing

At the beginning of your parent's hospital stay, they will be asked to fill out a form about the food preferences, dislikes and allergies. This is the one time you (and your parent) will see your parent's options, typically on a printed menu with available breakfast, lunch and dinner choices. From that point, they usually narrow down the options available further, depending on your parent's illness. Most of the time, they won't tell you everything they 'can' cook, including items absent from the menus, so be sure to ask what's possible.

While your parent will likely be on a special diet, you may still be able to request foods within that diet. I tried to stick to foods in their whole form with the least amount of processing, meaning unrefined or modified fruits, veggies, meat, fish, beans, and whole grains. Use these simple rules and your parent will have a better hospital food experience.

For breakfast, Dad always splurged and got pancakes, waffles, or dry toast with jam on the side plus cereal. If your parent is sensitive to sugar, request the waffles or pancakes with plain butter and a little jam instead, or just order eggs. Coffee or tea is fine.

For lunch or dinner, Dad always opted for soup, salad, and roast chicken or salmon and requested it plain or dry, in other words, no salty gravy, sauces or messes. (Dad would say "they can't mess it up.") If you don't request these things, they will never make it to your room.

Hospital commissaries produce mass quantities in advance and would rather provide something easier such as meatloaf, however chicken or fish provide more 'whole' nutrition. Dessert of any kind is fine, or request fruit.

A Caregiver's Perspective: Lexie

The easiest way I get grounded is to be out in nature—not quite an option when you're with your parent in a hospital room.

When you can't be outside, sit and take a pause. Put your hand on your belly. Take a deep breath. Quiet your mind, and welcome in that sense of grounding.

Visit, Visit, Visit

Whatever length of time your loved one stays in the hospital, long or short, visit as often as you can, every day if possible—even if you only go for 15 minutes.

Whenever Dad was in the hospital, my own disappointment often set in: *I can't believe I have to go to the hospital again, I have so many other things I have to do...* or *This is exhausting.* However, I was not the sick person suffering, my parent was. He was the one being poked and prodded and staying in the hospital.

As their child and caregiver, we need to stay present and mindful of our thoughts so we may be a positive force for Mom or Dad. Remind yourself you can still enjoy your own life while finding the little joys available as shared moments that come up unexpectedly. This is yet another time to serve. It's not easy for them, but parents often put on a brave face for their children.

Shake Off Dance

Before you head out to visit, leave your baggage at the door. Do what I call the "Shake Off Dance" before you head out to see them.

Literally do a dance where you jump up and down waving your arms around to get some movement in your body. Shake it up, then shake it off. Don't think about looking foolish. Don't make excuses such as *I don't have the energy*, or *I don't feel well.* Just repeat... "I am strong. I've got this. I am present and will do my best at nurturing (my parent) today."

Next, really feel your feet on the ground and stand tall, minding your posture. Repeat again: "I am strong! I've got this! I am here to serve today!"

Now go do your thing.

The Arrival

While every hospital is different, they all have gift shops and snacks at the very least. Plants and flowers are thoughtful, but my experience is that they get in the way of the nurses trying to do their job. If you feel strongly that option is best to cheer your parent up, consider a small plant as opposed to flowers. And make sure there is room around your parent's area before you splurge on something over the top. Or consider taking it home with you when you go.

Cards are great. They don't take up room and are pleasant reminders for your loved ones once you're absent. If you bring a present, sensible options include mini-stuffed animals or small, soft and cuddly items. If your parent is allowed sweets, bring them treats from a favorite place in the outside world, or pick up something at the hospital's restaurant or gift shop.

When you arrive at your parent's floor, let the staff and nurses know you are around and available. There may be a lot of noise and confusion when your parent is in the hospital. New circumstances may come up quickly. Sometimes change gets emotional, so try and stay calm, especially when decisions need to be considered and made.

FROM THE HEART

Aunt Penelope

It is a special caregiver that can be there to assist tenderly, compassionately, and lovingly while remaining fully present during the moments of a loved one's decline and eventual death.

For me this special person is my Aunt Penelope.

For two decades I have always been extremely grateful for the kindness she showed both of my parents during my mother's last week on earth. My aunt went running to the aid of my dad when he was worn out and nearly on empty at the end of *his* caregiving journey for my mom. I remember her presence had a significant impact at that time, and then she recently shared more details once I interviewed her for this book.

Her sage advice in her own words:

Lenny called me when your mother (Barbara,) was dying and he said "I am so tired, I haven't slept in four days. And she still has pain, and…"

I said, "I'll come, Lenny, I'll come."

Once I arrived, your dad was on his last legs: exhausted, fearful, and just so upset. I told him: "The most important thing is that every night I'm here, I am going to sleep right beside Barbara in the living room so you will be able to get back into your own bed and sleep the whole night."

All it took was someone who kind of knew the ropes to get everything organized so life could go on again, and that someone happened to be me. (Thank goodness, as I have cherished memories.) And so it went: everything got taken care of; the rhythm of the day got re-established. Your mother, relieved of her pain and nurses periodically making sure she was okay meant your dad got some sleep. The sun would rise, and the day's activities happened. Then the sun went down, and the night's activities began.

It is so important for rhythm to be re-established, because without rhythm there is disharmony, anxiety, anger, fear, not to mention exhaustion. Your Dad was able to cook again. That was his self-care. He loved to cook so much. Guests came over and Lenny made everyone his Italian specialties which brought a huge smile to his face.

So, re-establishing *the heartbeat of the day* is necessary for Presence. Not that unexpected things won't happen, but once a rhythm is in place, you can just ride the waves as they come in, one wave after the next. You just ride them out instead of them crashing over your head.

A Caregiver's Perspective: Amber

Sometimes when Mom and I go to bed, we just look at each other and I feel as though we're simply making peace with how things are without saying anything.

Not to sound morbid but it's temporary, right? I don't know what her timeframe is going to be.

Enrichment

* * *

(Author note: Please skip this section if it's not for you. I respect you no matter what your relationship with your parent is. The act of caregiving may be all you can do. I understand. You're doing it: being there for them the best you can. Thank you.)

* * *

AFFECTION

Touch: noun. A gentle push, tap, or caress. *-Dictionary.com*

You don't understand their vulnerability until you're in it, seeing your parent ill and deteriorating. Even when you're with them every day, it's still hard to believe, difficult to grasp and watch. Caregiving is hard. The circle of life is HARD. Eventually you see them as an innocent being and it clicks, although it's uncomfortable and feels awkward. We hesitate: *what to do?* Yet, what do we do with other vulnerable loved ones such as babies and toddlers? Hugs and kisses.

Hug your Mom or Dad. Even if that isn't something you did before, try it now. Squeeze them and tell them you love them. Try it. If they don't respond, it doesn't mean they don't love you, some individuals just have a hard time with physical affection, even in the end of their lives. All parents love their children. They may not know how to show it, but they love you.

Hold their hand. This simple and profound gesture helps everyone who is looking to connect. When I was in the throes of caregiving, I didn't understand why handholding was important (another reason I wrote this book: we all need reminders of acts of human compassion.) My Dad and I told each other we loved each other every day. It helped us both. Yet a friend's mom knew my dad was sick and said to me one day, "Don't forget to touch him". I thought, what is she talking about?

She explained, "Hold his hand or touch his feet, keep your hands on his feet for a good amount of time. Touch makes us feel connected, less lonely and afraid—it even reduces stress."

She was right; but I couldn't touch my dad's feet. Even in bed he didn't like his feet touched. Only Miss Shutes, the nursing home aide he adored, could wash his feet. Handholding, however, the small act of holding hands really touched Dad and me. We experienced that shared contact in our own special ways.

Sometimes in those final years when Dad was bedbound, I would also lie my head on his chest. I always felt safe just being in the room with him, sitting beside him. Putting my head on his chest provided comfort beyond words.

The last time I saw Dad, I longed to alleviate his extreme pain and was so frustrated there was no solution available. I understood what was unfolding and refused to leave his side—not for a minute. I asked him how I could possibly help and he reassured me, "Debs, there is nothing you can do."

So, I just leaned over from the chair, put my head on his chest, and we fell asleep together.

Remember your mantra.
Remember this doesn't last forever.
Don't forget to breathe.
I love you.

A Caregiver's Perspective: Susan

The whole role-reversal thing is a real mind game. Some people probably deal with
this better than others, though for me it was quite scary. It's so hard because this person's life is in your hands, and I never wanted to sign up for that.

My therapist kept telling me to "have compassion for yourself," "put the hammer down," "be kind to yourself," "don't have these unrealistic expectations," but, I tell you: just being able to put my head in my mother's lap when she was in the nursing home was so comforting.

A Caregiver's Perspective: Tyler

My biggest advice is to love on them. I think a lot of it has to do with the human touch since they can no longer communicate with you verbally to specifically say what they want to say.

Sitting next to them and leaning on them or putting your head on their shoulder, helps. Plus, multiple hugs. Hugs are my love language with Mom, now. She will hold on as tight as she possibly can and that's how I know she knows it's me.

Music & Singing

Music and singing are great ways to uplift our spirits, get out of our heads, and be present. What kind of music do Mom or Dad like? If they're impartial, try playing soft, rocking music and then something more lively to see what gets the better response. If we only focus on the day's tasks to help sick patients, we risk forgetting they are still alive. Whatever our state of health, humans *need* art, music, entertainment and community. Play some music and watch their spirits lift.

A Caregiver's Perspective: Tyler

I have been singing and dancing since I was 8 years old: Ballet, tap, modern, dance... Singing and dancing is huge for me and it has got me through all of this. Mom always encouraged me. My first job was as a kid dancing in one of Disney's Christmas parades!

My mom and I really enjoy singing together. When she lived with me before going into the care facility, I would put reruns of the show Glee on TV and my mom loved it. We would sing and dance all of the steps together!

Research shows humming also helps regulate the nervous system. Try humming when you're waiting for your parent in the doctor's office's lobby, or at a hospital while they're in or out of surgery or other treatments. It's a beneficial practice to stay grounded.

Lenny's Story: My Parents

My parents loved to tell the story of how they met on the dance floor (and especially how good lookin' they were.) City boy-meets-suburban-girl from Long Island equals love at first sight (or first dance.) "The Sunrise Village" hall was located on a main street in the town I grew up in. Apparently, it was ornately elegant and one of the mainstays for young singles to meet their mates. Of course, by the time I was born, *The Sunrise Village* had become a strip mall with a grocery store, pharmacy, yogurt shop and an Italian Restaurant called *Picollo* which became my parents' favorite restaurant. Can you believe it? It seems magical their favorite eatery was in the exact same spot where they met on the dance floor and fell in love decades earlier.

Mom and Dad would get giddy sharing stories of their love of dance and each other. Both were exceptional dancers, and I was proud to call them my parents at every wedding where we'd "get down and boogie" as a family. I remember it clearly: my father was an Italian rock star on the dance floor. By the end of the night, he would do a kind of strip tease, joking around and removing a few articles of clothing. Everyone gathered in a circle around him, clapping and chanting *"Lenny, Lenny."* After his jacket, tie, and a few buttons, his brothers would intervene screaming *"There are kids here!"* and tug him out of the spotlight. Dad would wrap with a few more gyrations to complete his dance act. Those were the most fun times I've ever had.

My mother loved to sing. She had a kitchen radio constantly playing the AM station with all the songs of the 70's. I loved hearing her sing all the wrong lyrics out of key. She was just happy washing dishes, or cutting potatoes to make her favorite food, (French fries). I can still see the yellow lace curtains and patterned orange wallpaper, and the plaque I loved that said *"This is my house and I will do as I darn please"* which summed up my childhood.

My dad also loved to sing, especially in the grocery store. (We did the shopping given my mom's condition.) He would always belt out a tune in the aisle and I'd groan "Dad, stop! You're embarrassing me!" but I secretly loved it. We had monumental fun; he was just so great to spend time with.

Resentment, Joy & Forgivness

Resentment

So many caregivers admit having to process role-reversal syndrome during their experience. I felt that with Dad a few notable times. It may sound strange, but because I didn't have children, at times it felt a bit as if *he* was my kid. It was just so hard to watch a man of his size shrink down as he did in the end: a six-foot, broad, larger-than-life man, reduced to...

Well, even when we are looking right at them lying there in a hospital bed or nursing home, it's uncanny how our mind plays tricks on us. We always see the person they once were.

I admit, there are times I felt resentful. I didn't resent him for the changes; I resented it just happening, period. It would last only for a day or two, until I was able to get grounded again by really caring for myself. I imagine it was also part of my coping mechanism—a way of dealing with the reality of it all.

Whenever you start to feel resentful, it's either because your plate is too full and you need to delegate more responsibility, or else your support team isn't big enough.

It's also a sign that you need to pause, take a breath, and step back. Meditation comes in handy, here; sometimes sitting with a thought is a good way to find answers. Ask yourself, *what am I missing? What do I need to feel good about my life or myself right now?* If you can get quiet enough to hear the answers, you may be surprised what comes in. The trick is not to force it.

Whenever we force our minds to deliver, it gives us quick solutions. So if we want the real truth and to get deeper into what we really need, we must allow things to unfold over whatever time it takes: minutes, hours, even days. Sometimes a quick answer works; other times, we wait. The idea is about the pause more than anything else. Get quiet. Grant yourself this time.

It's also okay to reject being a caregiver if you need to be honest with yourself. It really isn't a job for everyone. Try not to resent those people who want to do it differently (from your choices,) or those in your sphere who opt out, too. Also resist resenting anyone who thinks they have a choice that you don't believe you have. Instead, focus on the strong team you put in place and celebrate them.

The antidotes for Resentment are **Forgiveness, Gratitude and Joy.** Self-care allows you to feel rested, nourished, and prepared which give you access to the doorways to those antidotes.

A Caregiver's Perspective: Tyler

My advice? Just be patient. Alzheimer's is a very hard disease. It's emotional with a lot of ups and downs. Man, I've had days of just crying. Really. Being so frustrated with wanting to do more and help more... Sometimes you just can't do more. All you can do is just be there.

> No matter what, tell them "I'm doing this because I love you. You raised me. Now it's my turn to help you."

*Caregiving is so hard: maybe the
hardest thing you will ever do in your life.
Time is a true healer. Try to be patient.*

Joy

My dad was always the one keeping it light and having fun with our family. Once he got sick, he had a hard time keeping it light, as most do when they feel ill. The last few years he couldn't walk any longer, and in essence, he became helpless. Helplessness is an awful feeling. On top of that, he worried about his pain and what he was leaving behind. In a word: dying.

The guilt our parents feel when we give care to them is tremendous. They feel as if they are a burden, and on bad days, you feel it, too. That is okay. We are only human. The reason we take on caregiving is because we love them, and we accept that life works in a circle. They bring us into the world, do their best to give us care, and in turn we do the same.

While you are here on the journey of caregiving, let them know that you *want* to do this. Just as their encouragement helped you when you were young, hearing this helps them relax and feel at ease, and in turn you will too. While doing menial caregiving tasks, recite your mantra, hum a song, or heck—sing out loud. My Dad taught me that trick grocery shopping, so once I became caregiver to him, I returned the favor. I'd belt out loud as we pulled up to the doctor for his chemo appointments. And he laughed and laughed.

Energy is real. We don't usually consider how what we feel and what we think affects everyone around us. So, lightening up is part of our service work. Put that self- care in service to yourself so you can be the best version of yourself on this journey.

Remember that we are responsible for creating joy in our lives, good times and bad. It's okay to be light even when things aren't so joyous. Seize your chance to be the clown you always wanted to be. Go ahead have some fun. Make fun a bit, dance at the end of the bed, joke when it feels right... Give the sunniest side of yourself; it will make both parties' days shine.

Forgiveness
It was the worst day of my life.

I was in California on the phone with my dad in New York.

How could this be? How could I not get myself there in time! How can I beam myself into his hospital room right now?

To make matters worse, my brother was having surgery in a New York hospital at the exact time my dad was dying in a different New York hospital's ICU.

It felt so unfair and heartbreaking: the two that loved Dad most couldn't physically be there when he took his last breath. I *still* can't forgive myself, even though I spent four years dedicated to his daily care. Tears roll down my face writing about it almost three years since the day of his death. I think about it all the time.

I know the self-forgiveness will come, but...
It came so quick: Dad got sick again and was sent to the hospital. I was in California, so my brother was the one making daily hospital trips while I'd regularly fly back and forth. But that day,

neither of us could get there when Dad was suddenly rushed to the ICU.

The directives in place were "do not resuscitate"—Dad's wishes—however, in the heat of the moment they're asking me, *May we do this procedure and that procedure?* Wow. I panicked. What do you say? How do you say no? Regrettably, under pressure I said yes to just about everything, (which is why you *need* to have a talk with your parents early.)

Not knowing what else to do, I frantically called my best girlfriend, Cindy. I have known Cindy almost all my life. She still lived in the town I grew up in, near my dad. And she loved him. She was one of the amazing humans on our little team who visited weekly and brought him his favorite sandwich.

"Dad's not doing well! He is in the ICU, and Angelo is having surgery!"

The moment is so clearly etched in my mind forever. She said, "I am down the street leaving work. I can get there in ten minutes."

Oh, my God, really? Guilt, happiness, sadness—every emotion known to woman came over me. Honestly, mostly I felt afraid—no, make that terrified.

Cindy made it to the hospital and to my father's side just in time. She held his hand while I was on the phone with them. Then he took his last breath.

I still feel the guilt now and start to berate myself until my husband nips it in the bud: "You better stop it. You did everything you possibly could."

* * *

Ahhh, the prodigious act of forgiveness: the most difficult gift to give ourselves.

I needed to include this chapter because forgiveness is an enormous act of 360° care. Caregiving is complicated: It comes out of nowhere. It's convoluted, and rightfully so. You are just thrown into a role. Forgiving yourself for every misstep; forgiving your parent for taking you through this experience; forgiving anyone on your support team for disappointments... forgiveness is important.

Self-forgiveness may be the most difficult challenge you will ask of yourself. It really is part letting go, part self-love. If you are actively living, actively challenging yourself, you will come across a lot of opportunities to practice forgiveness and self-love.

Disease, distress, debilitation, they're all unexpected; they just happen. Caregiving is the same. There are no ways to prepare for its arrival. Although the minute you realize you're in it, you may arm yourself by understanding you can only do so much. Consider that everything you want to get done each day will probably only be a *wish* list. Forgive yourself each time you forget something, every time you get angry at Mom or Dad, and every time you think you did the wrong thing. Mistakes will be made.

You also need to forgive yourself for some of the unpleasant thoughts you may have regarding their lives or situations. Thoughts are just thoughts. They are not harmful. It's your actions that mean something in the end. Yes, we all want good thoughts to enjoy life and to project into our future goals and missions; but ultimately, thoughts should not run our lives. Let them go. (Remember your new meditation skills?) Clouds passing in the sky; let them float away...

The more you engage in life, the more forgiveness you will need to foster towards others and yourself. To be non-judgmental is a daily act of forgiveness. Acknowledge you had the courage to show up for this task at hand and do everything you are doing. How's *that* for a thought to dwell on? Think about having the courage to forgive yourself. Even if you disregard anything else in this book, do this one act: forgive yourself. Then forgive everyone. Be lighter so you might feel whole again.

I am prepared for my own guilt to finally subside and release; however, forgiveness is easier said than done. I am letting the Universe know that I am open and ready.

Saying Goodbye

A Caregiver's Story: Dr. Penelope Potter

When I was an attending doctor at a hospital in Sioux Lookout, Ontario, I had a patient in her late forties with breast cancer. At the time, the patient knew she was going to die and really wanted to go home. So, I let the family know that I would be available for whatever they needed and offered, "How about she goes home, and I will take care of her there?"

She went home Christmas Eve. Her status was getting lower and lower, so I went every day during that week to establish a rhythm of care. Her hospital bed was now set up in the living room so she could at least look out the east window. Each family member dutifully took on their roles: mealtimes, visiting times, sleep times... managing good pain control...

(That last one gets loved ones really upset, when their own loved one is in pain; although they don't like the patient being too drowsy, either. But sometimes it requires time to find the right medicine, the right dose, and establishing the right times.)

The family established their rhythm and were able to give consistent quality care to their mother. By New Year's Eve she was barely conscious, and despite trying to preserve a sense of normalcy, I sensed an incredible amount of anxiety surfacing.

I asked her husband, "What would you usually do on New Year's Eve?"

"We might crack a bottle of champagne and make a toast."

"I think you should go get that bottle of champagne." The son and father looked at each other and suddenly ran out the door. When they got home, the father said, "Can you believe it? We got the last bottle!"

"Of course!" I said, "That's because that was just for you."

The family and I sat around and celebrated New Year's Eve together. They told stories which restored that sense of normalcy. Around midnight, we got these little glasses out and cranked her bed up so she was just about sitting all the way up.

"Mom it's almost midnight and we're going to have champagne!"

The hour struck and they toasted each other. Her husband held the glass up to her mouth to put a little bit on her lips and I went home.
About 5 a.m., they called, "We think she's gone."
"Is she breathing?" I asked.

"Oh, yes. She just took a breath!"

"Okay, I will be right there."

She was still breathing when I arrived. Within another hour, she would occasionally stop breathing, but by then, this beautiful orange sun had started to rise. We watched through the east window as a golden light appeared and then illuminated the room.

A golden glow shone on her face just as she took her last breath.

This heartbroken family had one of the best New Year's Eves—and mornings—ever, simply because they had a chance to do what they all loved to do: come together and carry on. They knew they did absolutely everything they could up to the end for their beloved wife and mother.

It is important to remember that during those twilight moments, to make sure your person is included and you're not just talking around them. Even though they seem unresponsive, they can still hear you. You will see a faint smile or a hand move. No matter how small a gesture, know that life goes on.

Life goes on.

A Caregiver's Perspective: Lexie

Ya know, I just loved my mother. As difficult as caregiving is, I just loved her so dearly. There was just no way... I mean, I just *knew* I would do anything in my means to help her not suffer so much. Even a phone call to let her know that she wasn't being abandoned could bring a smile to her face.

So, when they called me from the foster care home where Mom was living and told me she had passed in her sleep during the night, I asked them to please not move her.

When we arrived, I thought it was important to bathe her, so I did just that. I gave her fresh clean clothes, combed her hair, put on a little cologne and some lipstick—all before the coroner got there. There were some flowers and I put them in her hands.

Holding grace for the person that's suffering is important. That means first holding grace for your parent and then for yourself.

A Caregiver's Perspective: Val

My grandmother was in her 90's when she passed. Near the end, she was becoming more helpless and began accepting all that we could give to her (and she also began to finally appreciate it). So, one day she said to me:

"Valerie, do you think the Lord forgot about me?"

"No."

"Well, I'm ready to go. Would you pray with me so that I can go?"

"Sure." And I did. I prayed with her. And she was gone within a few days.

A Caregiver's Perspective: Erin

When my dad had about six months to live, I was in a major car accident. My rear tire blew and the car flipped 7 times on the freeway. The steering wheel fractured most of my ribs, and multiple bones in my face and neck. My C2 broke and my C3 snapped, paralyzing me for the first 24 hours.

It turns out my dad and I were in the hospital at the same time. My poor mom had the love of her life dying of pancreatic cancer on one floor, and her only child laid up in the ICU with traumatic spinal cord and brain injuries.

Thankfully, my dad and I both returned home from the hospital to recover together and shoot for the next milestone, my birthday.

On my 28th birthday my dad pushed me to go to Vegas with my friends. He said, "Spike, (my nickname,) go enjoy your birthday with your friends!" He promised he would be there when I got back from the weekend. And he was.

Next, Dad made it through his wedding anniversary, then the holidays which he loved so much. However, almost immediately after the New Year, Dad started having high fevers and his health began to turn for the worst. Yet, on the 6th of January, I got a clean bill of health that I had fully healed from the accident—almost a medical miracle considering the severity and extent of trauma involved with my spinal cord injury.

Dad passed away on January 7th—the next day. It's as though he held on as long as he could until he knew I was okay.

Because of my accident, I spent 24 hours a day with my Dad the last six months of his life. I would absolutely break my neck all over again for that time with him.

A Caregiver's Perspective: Penelope

The last couple weeks of Mom's life she could no longer get into the tub, so I made a basin of hot bubbly water and carried it in to her room. It smelled fragrant so she opened her eyes, which were kind of sticky at that point.

"Oh, a bath!"

And I said, "A bird bath," which made her laugh, although being so weak, she coughed up phlegm.

As an old nurse by trade, she said "Penelope, let me see that." I handed her the tissue and she looked at the phlegm that held the classic pneumococcal discharge and said, "Penelope, I have pneumonia."

"Yes, Mom. Yes, you do."

Then she said, "I'm going home."

"Yes, Mom. You're going home. Who do you want to see first when you get there?"

"I want to see my momma."

OK, I am not crying with sadness; I am crying because it was such a beautiful, tender moment because my Mom's mother also died of pneumonia. It happened when my mother was in nurses' training in London, Ontario. She got the call at University that her mom was dying and got the earliest train home, but once she got there, her mother had already passed away.

> So, isn't that amazing? I ask Mom, who do you want to see? And she says, *I want to see my momma.*

Endings & Beginnings...

The ending never seems real. We can't face the ultimate truth, so we don't fully believe it. It's as if they're still there, in their chair, or their bed, waiting to have a conversation, to pick up the phone...

A couple weeks after Dad passed (or was it months?) I took myself to the most beautiful beach in Malibu, California. Whenever I see the *Welcome to Malibu* sign, I feel instant relaxation and an everlasting sense of serenity comes over me. (Southern California's high cost of living does have its occasional perks.)

I had a delicious breakfast at Malibu Farm, my favorite place overlooking the Pacific with its crashing waves to the left and surfers to the right of the pier. Afterwards, I proceeded on a slow, healing pace onto the sand for a long beach walk. I removed my shoes to feel the wondrous grains of sand between my toes. I felt connected and grounded, something I hadn't felt lately.

After a mile or so, I needed a break. I was still in recovery phase from Dad's passing, so I laid down on the sand, dropping my backpack under my head as a pillow. I didn't expect to fall asleep, but it was winter, so no one was around, and the temperature was a perfect 68 degrees.

I fell into a deep sleep; who knows how long I slept?

When I woke up, I looked out at the water where an entire pod of dolphins was jumping for joy in the air, one after the next, after the next. There must have been twenty, maybe more. All on their journey to Somewhere, jumping without a care in the world and living life.

Elated, I was so grateful for the moment. I just sat there staring out into the horizon for the longest time watching that wondrous sight, tears rolling down my face, enjoying every drop of that divine wink in time. What a perfect ending (beginning) to my next chapter.

I guess it's time to fully care for myself, now.

*　*　*

It's been three years since Dad has passed, and I have to say, I miss being his caregiver. I miss him. My life's work is caring for and about others and I appreciate helping others. More important, however, is that I know I'm not alone. Please know you're not alone, either.

Timing plays an enormous role in how things play out in life. Understand and accept this is your time to be a caregiver. As hard as it seems now, you will not have regrets. Regardless of anyone's relationship with their parents, our parents brought us into the world for a reason (perhaps simply to learn self-love while caring for them). Everything happens when it's supposed to. Accepting this simple concept may help you continue your role with more ease.

Through caregiving, you and I have both experienced something not everyone gets to experience in a lifetime. Mine has made me a more compassionate, loving human being. For me, the best things in life are community and connection: a good chat and spending time with the ones you love. Is there much more to strive for? We are all here to help one another. Without others' support, what are we really experiencing on our life journeys?

Thank you again for finding me and my contributors, and the handbook we've compiled to help guide you. There are no accidents, no coincidences. You found this book on purpose. I'm so glad you found us and that we found you, too.

Thank you for allowing us to go on this adventure together.

Be well, my dear.

With love + light,

Debra (Lenny + Barbara's daughter)

Made in United States
North Haven, CT
06 October 2022